Local Partnership:
A Successful Strategy
for Social Cohesion?

The European Foundation for the Improvement of Living and Working Conditions is an autonomous body of the European Union, created to assist the formulation of future policy on social and work-related matters.

This report has been written for the Foundation by Dr Mike Geddes, University of Warwick.

Dr Mike Geddes is Principal Research Fellow and Research Manager in the Local Government Centre, Warwick Business School, University of Warwick, UK. He has researched and written extensively on issues of local economic and social policy, including local economic development and regeneration, local policies to combat poverty and exclusion, and local public services and local democracy. He is co-Editor of *Local Economy,* the leading UK journal specialising in local economic development.

Local Partnership:
A Successful Strategy
for Social Cohesion?

EUROPEAN RESEARCH REPORT

Dr. Michael Geddes
University of Warwick

EUROPEAN FOUNDATION
for the Improvement of Living and Working Conditions
Wyattville Road, Loughlinstown, Co. Dublin, Ireland
Tel: +353 1 204 3100 Fax: +353 1 282 6456/282 4209
E-mail: postmaster@eurofound.ie.

The paper used in this publication is chlorine free and comes from managed forests in Northern Europe.
For every tree felled, at least one new tree is planted.

Cataloguing data can be found at the end of this publication

Luxembourg: Office for Official Publications of the European Communities, 1998

ISBN 92-828-3050-0

Printed in Ireland

Foreword

The Foundation's work programme on strategies to promote social cohesion in the European Union has underlined the implications of new institutional structures and changing roles of the key actors. New relationships and approaches have been captured in the term "partnership" which is now frequently used in European Union and national policy documents . Its specific meaning or form is not always clear but it points to an increasing need and demand for authorities and bodies to seek to collaborate with other organisations in order to achieve a mutually agreeable set of policy goals.

Many of the problems which are symptomatic of social exclusion (poverty, unemployment, marginalisation, social and economic stress), are interrelated and require a complex and coordinated policy response, drawing upon the skills and resources of a wide range of social actors. The fact that frequently such problems are also geographically concentrated - in specific neighbourhoods, urban and rural regions - has led to an increasing emphasis on a local dimension in policy responses. A third feature of such policy responses to social exclusion has been the call to involve and empower those citizens and residents affected by the problems in the development and implementation of the solutions. This flourishing of local partnership structures which seek to harness the skills and resources of actors from public authorities, the social partners (employers, trade unions), the voluntary sector and local citizens groups, has arisen from these trends. The active promotion of such a partnership approach within European Union and some national government programmes has also been an important factor in the growth of local partnership structures.

Much of the Foundation's own experience as a partnership type organisation as well as its previous research on social exclusion had pointed to the benefits of greater involvement and collaboration of the different parties concerned by these developments in European society. And yet the mechanisms or principles for successful partnership working and effective partnership strategies were unclear. Thus in 1994 we launched a cross-national analysis of the development of a local partnership approach to promote social cohesion; of the structures and working methods and of the contribution and impact of such bodies. It was felt that a European analysis of developments within different programmes, in different contexts and cultures, and involving a wide range of different partners and actors could assist in identifying effective practice, in improving the transfer of experience and reducing the waste of resources.

This report provides an overview of the results of 10 national studies and 5 smaller country reviews of developments and practice. It was evaluated in September 1997 by representatives of the Foundation's Administrative Board (governments, employers, trade unions, European Commission) and representatives of the European Parliament and OECD. They saw the research as presenting experiences and frameworks for development which would be useful to policymakers seeking more collective responses to social problems. It provided lessons which could be used in recent developments such as the territorial employment pacts and in the debate on the future of the Structural Funds. Particular points which were of interest were the key role of EU and national programmes in local partnership development; the need for more active involvement of the social partners; and for more attention to be paid to representation, accountability and evaluation.

Clive Purkiss   Eric Verborgh
Director   Deputy Director

Contents

■

Introduction

The structure of the report

Chapter 1 of the report is an introductory one. It describes the aims of the research, and sets these in the context of the current economic and social challenges facing the European Union and the Member States, indicating how local partnerships represent an increasingly important response to problems of unemployment, poverty and social exclusion. It outlines the issues upon which the research focuses, and how it was undertaken.

Chapters 2 and 3 then discuss the way in which a partnership approach, and local partnerships in the more specific sense with which the research is primarily concerned, have been developed in European Union policies and programmes (Chapter 2) and in different Member States (Chapter 3). The latter shows how the extent to which local partnerships have been developed varies considerably from one country to another, and outlines the main reasons for this.

Chapter 4, in contrast, presents an overview of the main features of all the local partnerships, 86 in all, identified in the research across the Member States of the EU, principally in the ten countries for which research reports were prepared, but also drawing on supplementary research for the other five Member States. It describes how these partnerships originated, in what kind of locations, which interests are involved as partners and how they are organised, the issues with which they are concerned, and their sources of funding.

On the basis of the overview provided in Chapter 4, Chapters 5 and 6 then analyse the contribution which local partnerships can make to policies to tackle unemployment, poverty and social exclusion, drawing on thirty detailed case studies undertaken in the ten main national research studies. Chapter 5 is concerned with the experiences at the local level in building effective partnership, reflecting the views of key actors in interviews undertaken in each case study. Chapter 6 then considers the impacts which local partnerships have achieved, both in promoting new ways of working and in their impact on unemployment and social exclusion.

Chapter 7 presents the conclusions and policy implications of the research. It summarises the main conclusions from the research, and outlines the proposals arising from them for those involved in partnerships at the local level, for the social partners and for the policies and programmes of national governments and at European level.

Chapter 1

The Scope and Context of the Research

Introduction

This chapter describes the research which has been undertaken and sets it in the context of the economic and social challenges facing the European Union. The rationale and aims of the research are outlined, noting that while the establishment of local partnerships has become increasingly widespread in recent years, there has been only limited evaluation and assessment of the effectiveness of the partnership approach, particularly on a cross-national and cross-programme basis. The emergence and potential contribution of local partnerships is then placed in the context of the EU's policy goals of social cohesion, integration and social inclusion and the challenges of unemployment, poverty and exclusion facing Europe. The final section of the chapter then identifies some of the major questions and issues about the partnership approach, and shows how the research has been designed to cast light on these.

The rationale and aims of the research programme

This report results from a transnational research programme conducted by the European Foundation for the Improvement of Living and Working Conditions on The Role of Partnerships in Promoting Social Cohesion, over the period 1994-1997. The Foundation's review of its work on issues of social cohesion over the past decade had recognised the growing importance of a local partnership approach, while noting that it raised a number of policy and research issues (Ball 1994). The aim of the research programme was therefore to assess the contribution of the partnership approach to combating problems of poverty and social exclusion at the local level, and to suggest guidelines for policy-makers for the future.

In many EU and Member State programmes aimed at building social cohesion and combating poverty, unemployment and exclusion, the establishment of local partnerships has gained increasing importance in recent years. The aim of such arrangements is to harness the energy, skills and resources of the key actors - such as public authorities, employers, trade unions, voluntary organisations and local community groups - in developing and implementing local regeneration strategies. These partnerships take different forms and their work tends to cover a broad range of social, economic and environmental policies. They often focus on a specific local area such as deprived urban neighbourhoods, underdeveloped rural regions, or neglected housing estates, as in the following examples.

The *Onyar Est* partnership in, was located in a deprived neighbourhood of a prosperous city. Supported by the EU's Poverty 3 programme, the partnership involved interests from the public sector at different levels, from the voluntary and community sectors and from the social partners, who had not previously adopted a collaborative approach to problems of unemployment and poverty. The partnership developed a multidimensional strategy which was particularly innovative in linking social and economic issues and actions.

The *South Kerry Development Partnership* is located in a remote rural area in Ireland which suffers severely from isolation, depopulation and the absence of employment opportunities. The partnership secured funding from different sources including Irish government programmes and the EU LEADER I programme to promote an integrated approach to rural regeneration and the promotion of enterprise. Actors involved in the SKDP included local and national public sector agencies, the social partners and community organisations.

The *North Tyneside City Challenge* partnership in England is implementing a major urban regeneration programme funded by the UK government's City Challenge programme, in a district which suffers severe long-term unemployment caused by the decline of key industries such as shipbuilding and includes several depressed public housing estates. The partnership includes representatives of the local authority, other public and quasi-public agencies, business, voluntary organisations and community representatives.

However, while the principle of local partnership is now quite widely accepted, there remain too few examples of partnerships which can demonstrate lasting impact in tackling poverty and social exclusion on a broad and multidimensional basis. Relatively little evidence is available about the advantages and disadvantages of different models and structures of partnership, and about the outcomes for different partners and stakeholders, including both those directly involved in local partnerships and those who have a wider interest in the success of such local initiatives. Moreover, while there have been a number of evaluations of specific programmes and partnerships at European, national and local levels, there has been little previous cross-national and cross-programme assessment of the partnership approach. In this context, the objectives of this transnational research programme were:

- to document and assess the extent to which the local partnership approach is being adopted within EU Member States in programmes concerned with promoting social cohesion.

- to document and analyse the perceptions of public, private, voluntary and community partners concerning the impact of such partnerships and the problems they have encountered.

- to develop guidelines and recommendations to assist policy-makers and other interested parties in the future development of partnerships aimed at tackling social exclusion.

The research adopted a specific working definition of local partnerships, in order to distinguish them from more limited and/or informal processes of collaboration and networking, and to guide identification of suitable partnerships for the case study element of the research. The definition adopted emphasised four key features of local partnerships:

- A formal organisational structure for policy making and implementation

- The mobilisation of a coalition of interests and the commitment of a range of different partners

- A common agenda and multi-dimensional action programme

- To combat unemployment, poverty and social exclusion and promote social cohesion and inclusion.

Within the transnational research programme, research studies were undertaken in ten Member States of the EU: Austria, Belgium, France, Finland, Germany, Greece, Ireland, Portugal, Spain, and the United Kingdom. Details of the national research reports are given in Appendix I. In addition, supplementary research was undertaken for the remaining five Member States to ensure that the research was as comprehensive as possible in its coverage within the resources available. The research has been undertaken through a collaborative process. Regular research meetings between the Foundation and the national research teams (Appendix IIa) were held to develop the methodology, and discuss the findings and conclusions from the national research reports. Members of the Co-ordination Group contributed to the research from the perspectives of public policy makers, the social partners, and other interests. (Appendix IIb)

The economic and social challenges facing the European Union

The process of European economic integration, propelled by the creation of the Single Market, is associated with a new impetus to economic growth, but also with the emergence of new patterns of unemployment, poverty and social exclusion as economic and other changes impact in different ways on regions, localities and neighbourhoods. It is against this background, with its implications for social cohesion and inclusion, that the concept of partnership is increasingly being introduced into the policies and programmes of the European Union and Member States.

The economic and social challenges facing the Union stem from three broad processes:

Economic and industrial restructuring

Over the last ten or fifteen years, the European economy has encountered new challenges to its competitiveness in a more globalised world economy, while at the same time suffering the impact of successive recessions, with fragile intervening periods of economic growth. There has been a major economic shift from manufacturing to services; the introduction of new less labour-intensive production methods; and an increase in low-paid, part-time, temporary, casual and insecure work.

Trends such as these have produced higher and longer-lasting unemployment, and mean that poverty and economic insecurity are experienced by a significant number of those in work as well as those without jobs. These economic problems have led the EU to develop new strategies for economic growth, competitiveness and employment (European Commission 1993b, 1995b), including a new emphasis on the contribution of local development initiatives (European Commission 1994b, 1995a).

A crisis of welfare and public services

Demographic and social changes (including the weakening of the nuclear family and extended family networks; the increasing numbers of lone parent families, especially young single jobless parents; increasing homelessness; the ageing of the population) mean that there are new social groups experiencing poverty and social exclusion, putting greater pressure on welfare systems. At the same time, the collapse of stable economic growth and high levels of unemployment have undermined the tax base of post-war welfare regimes. These pressures have stretched public agencies to, and sometimes beyond, the limits of their ability to meet needs. In some places the inability of the welfare system to cope has been reflected in community breakdown, expressed in outbreaks of crime, riot and disorder. These problems have led the European Union and Member States to explore new directions for social policy (European Commission 1993a, 1994a), for social welfare and social protection (Cousins 1997) and public services (Deakin, Davis and Thomas 1995).

Political participation and citizenship

Challenges to traditional patterns and processes of political representation and policy formulation have reflected a widespread disillusionment with established political parties, the limitations of representative democratic mechanisms and a growing interest in, and more demand for, the more direct involvement of citizens in the political and policy process (Chanan 1992). In some countries, established patterns of consultation between the social partners have been weakened or found inadequate in coping with new problems. Many commentators detect a shift of political and policy activity away from the nation state, both upwards to European institutions and downwards to the regional or local level.

Unemployment, poverty and social exclusion

The consequence of these rapid, complex and profound changes has been that:

"While the majority of Europe's citizens have benefited with increased opportunities and improved living and working conditions, a significant and growing minority have suffered poverty, unemployment and various other forms of social and economic disadvantage. They have been variously termed the excluded, the marginalised, or an underclass which possesses one or more disadvantages that restrict their ability to cope with and master change." (Ball 1994).

During most of the 1990s the number of people employed in the EU has declined, and unemployment remains stubbornly high, at 10.6% in mid-1997. Youth unemployment at over 20% is twice as high as that for adults, and long term unemployment, the most intractable element of the European unemployment problem, stands at over 50% of the total. The rate of unemployment for women remains considerably higher than that for men, at 12.5% compared with 9.3%. Moreover the incidence of unemployment has become much more uneven across the Union, both between and within the Member States. Deep recessions in some countries, such as Finland and Sweden have led to an absolute decline in employment, and unemployment has also increased in Spain and Greece despite the fact that these latter countries have created jobs at a higher rate than the average. In Ireland overall employment has been growing, while in countries such as Portugal, Belgium and the UK unemployment has been reduced. Because of the rise in participation, the growth of employment in 1996 was accompanied by a rise rather than a fall in unemployment, unlike in 1995. Over the two years of slow recovery, 1994-96, employment in the Union rose by around $1^1/_2$ million, not enough to reduce unemployment if participation had risen at its pre-1991 rate. As it was, unemployment fell, though by only 250,000. (European Commission 1997e)

High rates of unemployment and especially long-term unemployment are the dominant factors associated with poverty. In 1993, 57 million people in the European Union fell below the official poverty line of 50% of the average per capita income in each country (Eurostat, 1997), and poverty is considered to be increasing in the 1990s, leading to a growing polarisation of European societies (Abrahamson and Hansen, 1996).

As with unemployment, poverty is very unevenly distributed according to socio-economic characteristics, such as age, gender and household composition, and also according to place. High **rates** of poverty are found in regions of Europe with a large share of the population still employed in agriculture, ie in the southern and western countries of Ireland, Portugal, Spain, Italy and Greece. Socio-economic groups likely to experience poverty include the self employed, low skilled workers, women and immigrants/ethnic minorities. Transfer payments from the welfare system may also be minimal for groups such as young unemployed people, single parents, and the elderly.

The largest *numbers* of the poor (more than two thirds) are to be found though within more industrialised countries. In countries such as the UK, Germany, France and (northern) Italy, economic restructuring and de-industrialisation have caused unemployment, poverty and social exclusion in large cities and old industrial areas particularly. The most vulnerable are those with low or outdated skill levels, including high proportions of women, older workers and ethnic groups.

Unemployment and poverty is therefore now widespread across the European Union: in formerly prosperous as well as traditionally depressed regions; in the urban periphery as well as the inner city; in small and medium-sized towns as well as old industrial areas and large cities. In such areas, it has become recognised that there is an accumulation and combination of several types of deprivation which go beyond poverty to *social exclusion*: lack of education, deteriorating health conditions, homelessness, loss of family support, non-participation in the regular life of society, and lack of job opportunities. Each type of deprivation has an impact on the others. The result is a vicious circle (European Commission 1997d). The concept of social exclusion is intended to recognise not only the material deprivation of the poor, but also to their inability to fully exercise their social, cultural and political rights as citizens. It suggests that where the material living standards and citizen rights of significant numbers of people are restricted by persistent, multiple and concentrated deprivation, social cohesion is threatened.

As the concept of social exclusion has become more widely accepted, this has involved important shifts in perspective:

* from an exclusive focus on income poverty to a wider view of multidimensional disadvantage;

* from a static picture of states of deprivation to a more dynamic analysis of processes;

* from a focus on the individual or household to a recognition that it is also within communities that disadvantage is experienced (Berghman 1992; Room 1994).

The concept of exclusion highlights the idea of distance within society between the 'haves' and the 'have nots', and points towards the role of those who are creating exclusion, as well as those who are suffering it. It relates also to groups of people - ethnic minorities, women, elderly people, disabled people - who might not be considered to be outside the mainstream of society simply on an income definition of poverty.

Social cohesion, integration and inclusion

If exclusion processes are multidimensional in nature, "then preventing and combating social exclusion calls for an overall mobilisation of efforts and combination of both economic and social measures. At European level, this implies that social exclusion should be addressed in the framework of all Union policies" (European Commission 1994c, p49). The mandate to tackle exclusion has recently been strengthened through the provisions of the new Amsterdam Treaty (Council of the European Union, 1997).

The objective of **social cohesion** implies a reconciliation of a system of organisation based on market forces, freedom of opportunity and enterprise with a commitment to the values of internal solidarity and mutual support which ensures open access to benefit and protection for all members of society. The cohesion objective is recognised to have a specific geographical dimension of reducing disparities between the levels of development between the different parts of the Union and assisting the more disadvantaged areas and social groups, including the long-term and young unemployed and the poor. These imbalances - in particular those of unequal access to employment opportunities and rewards of work in the form of incomes - do not just imply a poorer quality of life for disadvantaged areas and groups, but an under utilisation of human and economic resources. Success in meeting the cohesion objective requires change to produce 'positive convergence' outcomes for the poorer regions and disadvantaged groups, not a reduction in growth or jobs for others (European Commission 1997a).

Policies for labour market **integration** are central to securing the cohesion objective. It is for this reason that, since the Essen European Council in December 1994, the Member States have been committed to a European Employment Strategy based on interrelated measures to enhance employment creating growth, social solidarity and equality, including special measures to promote access to jobs for the most vulnerable groups in the labour market. The Confidence Pact for Employment of November 1996 brought this strategy a step forward, by mobilising all those involved in the job creation process, especially the social partners. An important element of employment policy is the promotion of initiatives at regional and local level, including Territorial Employment Pacts referred to in the Confidence Pact (European Commission 1996b).

While more effective economic and labour market integration policies are crucial to disadvantaged areas and social groups, the multidimensional nature of

■

social exclusion means that other parallel policy action is also necessary to promote **social inclusion.** Social inclusion 'turns the concept of social exclusion on its head', by referencing to the 'positive side of the same coin that also contains social exclusion' (Walsh et al 1997) and encapsulates the process whereby all members of a society are enabled to participate in its social, economic and civil activities. The term inclusion also emphasises the need for collective, corporate action, which enables people who have little or no experience of participation, or who are disillusioned with what they have experienced, to become involved in activity, debate and decision making (Henderson 1997). The objective of inclusion therefore relates to a number of policy areas, including policies to promote and extend social and political citizenship rights. The current debate about the future of social protection policy, launched by the EU at the end of 1995 with a discussion document on The Future of Social Protection (European Commission 1995d), indicates the continuing commitment of the EU to try to find innovative ways to respond both to the growth of poverty and social exclusion, and to the new pressures on social welfare systems. It is increasingly recognised that this cannot be achieved within a dual society in which wealth creation by a highly qualified workforce provides the basis for income transfers to a growing number of non-active citizens, but will require a more active society with a wider distribution of opportunities (European Commission 1994a). Key strands of the debate about the implications of an **'active society'** model concern:

- the search for active labour market policies which link economic and social objectives of welfare and work;

- the extension of mixed market models of welfare involving new relationships between public, private and voluntary sectors;

- the need for new relationships between local, national and European action, which can enhance the contribution of local authorities and local initiatives while avoiding the dangers of an over-localisation of policy responses.

The contribution of local partnerships to cohesion, integration and social inclusion

Current policy debates about cohesion and integration, and about economic development and social protection, show that considerable importance is being attached to a partnership approach and to the local dimension of policy action in European policies.

The local partnership approach appears to reflect policy recognition of :

- the multidimensional causes of unemployment, poverty and social exclusion

- the concentration of such problems in particular local communities and neighbourhoods, and among specific social groups

- the many actors involved and implicated in the success or failure of the attempts to combat unemployment and achieve greater cohesion, including different levels of government, the social partners, non-governmental organisations, local communities and excluded groups themselves.

In its second report for 1992, the European Observatory on National Policies to Combat Social Exclusion commented that "the debates about social exclusion are, as much as anything, debates about the new partnerships which must be forged within our European societies" (Robbins 1992). Partnership is of course not new: it builds on a history of inter-agency collaboration and participation by local communities in the implementation of programmes and the delivery of services in many countries. Nonetheless the current focus of policy debate around partnership reflects a widespread recognition that traditional social policies, of either a sectoral nature (eg housing, health, education) or targeted on specific social categories (women, the elderly, the young, those with disabilities, ethnic groups and migrants) must be supplemented by a more integrated and multidimensional approach, reflecting the complex causes of social exclusion. The current interest in partnership:

- entails a search for a more pluralist and flexible approach to problems which can transcend the remit of specific agencies and existing structures: both a break with traditional policy paradigms and a platform for policy innovation.

- seeks to overcome the compartmentalisation of policy issues inside the domains of separate agencies and services, and the paternalism and hierarchy associated with traditional policy mechanisms.

- seeks to facilitate new alliances and ways of understanding and reacting to problems; the sharing of risks and responsibilities in a changing and unpredictable policy environment; and an emphasis on lateral, local, inter-organisational and interpersonal networks as the basis for policy innovation.

Moreover, policies need to focus especially on those neighbourhoods and local communities where problems of poverty, social exclusion and unemployment are concentrated, and within which exclusion is experienced by individuals and families. An integrated approach to social exclusion through local partnership is therefore seen to offer the prospect of bringing together institutions and local communities to create new alliances, strategies and policy innovation against social exclusion.

The research programme: issues and methods

The local partnership approach is therefore seen to bring a number of possible advantages. An important rationale for the research has been that certain problems and limitations are becoming increasingly apparent, alongside the need for more evidence of the experience of partnership in different programmes and contexts. The **main questions and issues** about partnership can be summarised as follows:

* The current emphasis on partnership can involve a good deal of rhetoric. The differences between collaboration, consultation and partnership are not always clear. There are important questions about who should be involved in local partnerships concerned with unemployment, poverty and exclusion; and about how partnerships should be organised, with a need to assess the advantages and disadvantages of different structures and ways of working. What is the 'added value' which a partnership approach at the local level can bring, and what are the potential costs for those involved?

* Effective partnership requires the identification of mutual interests, the negotiation of a common strategy and agenda of action, and the commitment of mutual resources. To do so can mean managing a number of potential points of conflict. While partnership may assume a shared commitment to the norms and ways of working in partnership, partners will bring different values and cultures into the partnership, and these differences will assume particular importance at times of conflict. Power and resources are unlikely to be evenly distributed within partnerships, and partners may also derive differing degrees of influence from their organisations' external power and resources.

* The ability of partnerships in managing such conflicts is a central question for the partnership approach to problems of social exclusion, where the objective is the diffusion of power and resources towards less favoured areas and social groups, and where it cannot be assumed that there is an

a-priori convergence of interests between the potential partners. What has been the record of local partnerships in involving and empowering local communities and excluded groups, especially the most disadvantaged?

• More needs to be known about the impact and outcomes of local partnerships, both in contributing to solutions to problems of unemployment, poverty and social exclusion, and in contributing to policy innovation. To what extent have partnerships realised the expectations and objectives of the various organisations and interests involved? What kind of time horizons are needed for partnerships to be established and achieve results? How far have partnerships been able to develop and implement more effective multidimensional strategies? How effectively have the activities undertaken by partnerships been evaluated?

• Many of the programmes which have supported local partnerships have been either experimental in nature or limited in scope and/or resources. There are therefore important questions about how the experiences gained in pilot and experimental programmes can be transferred to mainstream policy and action. How can the experiences of individual local partnerships be shared more effectively so that good practice is disseminated at the grassroots, and how can those local experiences be integrated into wider policy networks and programmes?

• A further dimension is added to such questions by the important differences between Member States. In some countries (the UK and Ireland for example) the practice of local partnership is more widely understood because of the impact of national government programmes. In other countries (Spain, Portugal or Greece, for example) the usage is much less widespread, and is still quite closely associated with EU programmes rather than national policies. In yet others, the term partnership is primarily associated with corporatist type collaboration between government and the social partners, rather than between local actors and interests. In some countries, there are different terms conveying important parts of the concept, for example referring to formal institutional partnership and informal 'community' partnership.

The central concern of the research has been to explore questions such as these, and to identify the specific contribution which partnership can make to policies to combat poverty and exclusion:-

■

- In what ways, and in which circumstances, have partnerships produced better focused and more co-ordinated action, and innovative policy approaches, as a result of combining the contributions of a range of partners?

- Which ways of working seem to have been most effective in reaping the benefits and minimising the costs of partnership working?

- Where and how have local partnerships demonstrated success in developing agreed strategies and action plans, between public, private and voluntary sector actors?

- What can be learned from the less successful experiences?

- What conflicts and problems have partnerships encountered, and how have they sought to overcome them?

The methodology for the research programme was thus developed with the following objectives in mind:

- the need to understand the different circumstances bearing on the development of local partnerships in each Member State, but also to gain an overview of wider trends across the European Union;

- the need to survey a considerable number of local partnerships, in order to gain a grasp of the different approaches and experiences which exist, but also to analyse in depth how partnerships actually work, and what the experience of different partners and stakeholders actually has been.

To meet these objectives, the ten main national research studies have included three elements:

- **A review of the history and origins of the partnership approach in each country**; the current national policy context for local partnerships; and of the views of leading policy makers and actors about the partnership approach in the country concerned. Each national review also describes a number of partnerships (6-8) which illustrate important issues and trends in the country concerned. Together with the supplementary research on the countries not covered by major research studies, this means that the research identified 86 local partnerships spread across the EU. Summary information for all of these is presented in Appendix III.

- **Case studies of three local partnerships** in each of the ten main research studies (and therefore 30 in all), chosen to illustrate recent national experience, including successes but also problems encountered. These case studies were carefully chosen to provide detailed analyses of the operation of local partnerships in different spatial and socio-economic contexts: eg inner city, peripheral housing estates, rural areas; supported by a wide range of EU and national programmes, to illustrate a range of partnership structures and relationships involving public agencies, employers, trade unions and the voluntary and community sector, and to ensure coverage of important issues, such as gender and equal opportunity perspectives.

- **Conclusions and recommendations** for policy makers at European, national and local levels and for those directly involved in local partnerships concerned with problems of unemployment, poverty and exclusion.

It proved necessary at the beginning of the research to establish a common framework for identification of the wide range of interests, organisations and actors likely to be involved in local partnerships, as the way in which these may be described varies between countries. Different 'partners' also have contrasting stakes in, and views about, local partnerships. These are as follows:

The public sector

The public sector, including national government departments and agencies; local and regional governments, including both elected politicians and officials; other public sector or quasi-public agencies (concerned with education or training for example); public sector industries or utilities.

For many policy makers in the public sector, partnership is a corollary of the constraints on the sector's resources, and its more limited capacity for unilateral action. Increasingly however public authorities are recognising the gains to be made from proactive involvement in partnerships, and are seeking to play active and leading roles in local partnerships. Different public agencies vary in their resources and constraints, and their ability to be flexible when participating in partnerships. They look to partnerships to help them meet local needs, but also to help resolve their own problems. They are constrained by limited resources of both money and time. Public agencies with specific and defined functions may be challenged by the flexibility required in agreeing and implementing a common agenda.

Employers

Employers, including employer organisations (locally or more broadly-based); locally-based firms; externally-based firms with local interests; farmers' organisations; chambers of commerce.

The nature and commitment of private sector interests can range from large-scale commercial and development interests to smaller and more locally-based firms. Some private sector partners will be looking to partnerships as a source of commercial opportunities, through access to or subsidy for development schemes, while others may regard participation as a way of 'giving something back to the community', or in terms of public relations and local goodwill. However in some deprived areas the absence of significant private sector activity in the local economy may make it difficult to find committed private sector partners. The increasing involvement of business and employers in partnerships is raising questions about the ways in which employer interests are represented, and the relation between the role played by individuals and individual companies, and the employer and business interest more generally.

Trade unions

Trade unions, including local trade union organisations and individual trade unionists.

Trade unions have a valuable role to play in local partnerships, in contributing their experience of local employment issues and negotiation processes. Local partnerships can offer a framework in which the common interests of the employed workforce and the unemployed can be addressed jointly. However, local partnership may run counter to some trade unions' preference for national-level policy making, so that partnerships may not find it easy to attract official trade union participation. In some countries, trade union participation in partnerships has not been encouraged in the same way as that of employers and the private sector.

The voluntary sector

The voluntary and not-for-profit sector covers a wide range of organisations, from large national (and indeed transnational) organisations, such as churches and major charities, to small local voluntary organisations and associations. Voluntary organisations also fulfil different roles, from those of representation and advocacy on behalf of specific social groups, to - increasingly in many countries - provision of services. In many countries, voluntary agencies are now recognising the multidimensional nature of poverty and developing broader approaches in partnership with local communities and the public and private sectors.

The voluntary sector can play a key role in partnership, for example through the focus of some voluntary agencies on some of the most excluded social groups such as the homeless. Some voluntary sector organisations may also be less bound by formal rules than public agencies and therefore have potential for innovation and experiment. On the other hand, partnership working can result in a closer convergence between the public sector and voluntary agencies, especially the larger, more bureaucratised and professionalised ones.

The community sector

The community sector, including a wide variety of local community organisations from sports clubs to community businesses, and individual community representatives and activists.

Community partners contribute their direct experience of conditions in local areas and, often, their own strategies for change. While they do not bring significant financial resources to partnerships, they frequently make important commitments of time and energy. The way in which local community interests are represented, both in terms of the ability of community 'representatives' to speak on behalf of local people, and in terms of the strength of their representation within partnership structures vis-à-vis other interests, will often have an important influence on the extent to which partnerships meet local needs and offer real empowerment to the disadvantaged and excluded.

These categories are not always watertight. Public sector bodies may be active in partnerships as employers as well as in relation to their other functions. Local voluntary organisations often play an important role in representing 'community' interests. However as far as possible this report employs these categories of 'partners' in the following chapters.

Chapter 2

Partnership in European Union Policies

Introduction

This chapter describes the ways in which a partnership approach has been developed within European Union policies and programmes, considering both the emergence of partnership relationships in a broad sense, and local partnerships in (or close to) the definition adopted in the research. It draws upon documentary evidence and on research conducted in the course of this project, including a limited number of interviews with policy makers in the European Commission and with other important interests and actors at European level.

In the search for new and more effective responses to the growth of poverty, unemployment and exclusion, one of the new strategies which has emerged in the European Union has been the promotion of closer collaboration and joint working between different agencies and actors (from the public, private, voluntary and community sectors) and between different levels of government (European, national, regional and local). 'Partnership' has quickly become one of the key words in the vocabulary of the European Union, both in relation to policy responses to problems of unemployment and exclusion, but also more widely in searching for new ways of coping with profound economic, social and political change. The concept of partnership is however used in many different ways, and is rarely defined very precisely. It is employed generally, alongside words like cohesion, solidarity and subsidiarity, in European documents and discussions, to convey the kind of collaborative relationships which the European Commission is trying to develop with many different organisations.

Initially, 'partnership' in the European Community was conceived in fairly formal terms, as constitutional or institutional relationships between formal representative bodies, primarily at supra-national level. This has been evident in its early history and in its Institutions, such as the Economic and Social Committee (ECOSOC) which provides a formalised channel for views from social partners and other key social actors. This type of 'partnership' at European level was a reflection and expression of the pacts between capital, labour and the state, which had been negotiated within the Member States as part of the post war settlement. This corporatist concept has persisted (and been expanded in the post-Maastricht Social Dialogue) at European level while it has been challenged by a 'free market' philosophy in some of the Member States.

More recently partnership-type approaches have been both broadened and deepened within the EU, to the extent that during the 1990s a partnership approach has become a key feature of the EU's mainstream policies and programmes over a very wide field. It was enshrined as a principle within the 1988 Reform of the Structural Funds, and confirmed at the Lisbon Council. It was reinforced by the Maastricht Treaty commitment to strengthening the role of the social partners, and establishing the Committee of the Regions as a consultative body. The European Parliament has recorded its support for a partnership approach to local development, for example with reference to the Commission's proposals for territorial employment pacts, where "broad local alliances between public authorities, private organisations, the social partners and the population seem particularly well suited" (European Parliament 1997).

The principle of partnership has therefore now been extended beyond the traditional consultation with the social partners to embrace other tiers of government, and to include the national, regional and local authorities in new forms of co-operation and to include a wider range of bodies outside government, from the public, private, voluntary and grassroots sectors. This extension of partnership-type relationships has been driven by **financial, operational and developmental factors:**

- Many of the Commission's main programmes depend upon **co-financing** by the Member States or regional and local authorities.

- Partnership is one way of recognising the different stakeholders within the **monitoring and control** arrangements for the implementation of European Union policies on the ground;

- Partnership can produce added value from the European Commission's point of view by enabling local projects and actors to collaborate with other partners in innovatory projects and learning networks, transmitting knowledge and experience rapidly between the different 'partners' and across Member States.

Partnership in the Structural Funds and social action programmes

Partnership principles are now important in the mainstream Structural Funds, in the Community Initiatives, and in social action programmes such as the previous Poverty 3 programme. In the Structural Funds, the principle of partnership is closely linked to that of subsidiarity and a recognition of the advantages of decentralisation, involving the relevant authorities at all levels, and the social partners, in the pursuit of agreed objectives and the sharing of responsibilities for decision-making, including the involvement of those at the grassroots nearest to the problems for which solutions are being sought (European Commission 1997a).

In the mainstream Structural Funds, the main arena for a partnership approach is in the Monitoring Committees, which bring together European Commission, national government and regional and local officials and representatives of the social partners. These are now seen to be beginning to contribute creatively to problem analysis and to the local implementation of new Community guidelines and priorities, although the situation differs considerably between different Member States. In some cases, a clearer distinction between decision-making and consultative partners is seen to be desirable. A basic need though is for "information on the functioning of partnerships in practice and, by analysing this, ...to identify best practices and their transferability" (European Commission 1997a, p121).

In the Community Initiatives and social action programmes the Commission has been in a position to promote wider 'horizontal' partnerships among local actors. A wide range of programmes and Initiatives, such as Poverty 3, LEDA, LEADER, URBAN, INTERREG, NOW, Youthstart, HORIZON and INTEGRA, have promoted both a local partnership framework and transnational networks of local partnerships. URBAN, for example, offers financial support for development programmes for limited parts of cities, which are intended to address economic, social and environmental problems in a more comprehensive way, through integrated programmes based on local partnership.

The Commission takes a generally favourable view of the development of partnership in the Community Initiatives, regarding the fostering of co-operation and the formation of new partnerships, the generation of a spirit of experimentation and innovation, the encouragement of a grassroots, 'bottom up' approach and the dissemination of good practice as their strengths. However, it also considers that experience has been varied, with three Initiatives

- INTERREG, LEADER and URBAN - succeeding best in translating their objectives into effective action, strengthening the integrated nature of local development policies and having a mobilising effect on the ground, and adding value to Community cohesion policies (European Commission 1997a, p111-2).

A large number of the partnerships discussed in this research have participated in one or more of the Community Initiatives. Examples of these are:

LEADER I: GALCOB, Brittany; South Kerry, Ireland; IN LOCO, Portugal; Western Isles and Skye and Lochalsh, UK.

INTERREG: El Ribeiro, Spain.

NOW: West Attica, Greece; Tallaght, Ireland; Porto, Portugal.

HORIZON: Limerick, Ireland; Porto, Portugal

The European Poverty Programmes

In the context of local partnership to tackle social exclusion, the Poverty programmes were of particular importance in developing the European Commission's thinking and policy over a period of two decades. In 1974, in the wake of the oil crisis, the European Council recognised the need to address the growing problem of poverty. A year later the Commission launched its first programme of pilot studies to combat poverty (1975-1980). In practice these were not so much "studies" (research was brought in very late and could only be retrospective) as small-scale grassroots community action projects to tackle the immediate welfare needs of the most disadvantaged, such as the homeless (Commission of the European Communities 1989).

The second European Programme to Combat Poverty (1984-88) adopted a more structural and categorical definition of 'new poverty' (eg long term unemployment, rural poverty, ageing and elderly people), and involved agencies with some capacity to take action to resolve problems, not simply to voice them (eg national government agencies, local authorities and voluntary organisations as well as grassroots community groups).

The concept of new poverty which prevailed in the second European programme was replaced in the early 1990's by that of exclusion and integration. The title chosen for the Third European Programme (1989-1994) was " a medium term programme to foster the economic and social integration of the least privileged groups." Poverty 3 adopted an approach which was crystallised around three core principles of multidimensionality, partnership and participation.

In the Poverty 3 programme, partnership was required in terms of the composition and structure of the formal management committee (Partnership Board) for each of the local Model Action projects, bringing together a number of organisations (eg local authority, central or regional governments, universities, churches, and voluntary organisations) in a formal partnership board or committee, to share overall responsibility for steering the project, for managing the finances and hiring staff. Local partnerships were promoted within Poverty 3 as a particularly effective strategy for tackling multi-dimensional poverty and exclusion, cutting across the horizontal divisions which traditionally separate public and welfare services (eg jobs, income, housing, health, education, transport, leisure etc), and the solutions to which transcend the vertical divisions which separate different levels of government.

> Local partnerships considered in this research which participated in the Poverty 3 programme include the following:
>
> Charleroi, Belgium; Mantes, France; Friedrichshain, Germany; Thisseas, Perama, Greece; Limerick, Ireland; Porto and Guarda, Portugal; Girona and Montes de Oca, Spain; Granby-Toxteth and Brownlow Community Trust, UK.

Poverty 3 documents defined the benefits of local partnerships in terms of :-

- Co-ordination of policies, programmes and activities between different actors and agencies;

- Pooling of skills, resources and budgets between different organisations;

- Cross-fertilisation of creative ideas for innovative action;

- Sharing of the risks in experimental/pilot projects;

- Leverage of additional resources from external bodies (eg national governments);

- Political clout in lobbying central governments and mainstream bodies.

A number of requirements for effective local partnerships were also identified:-

- The development of shared vision and values between all the partners;

- Careful negotiation of a joint strategy and programme of action;

- Election or nomination of a leader who is trusted and respected both inside and outside the partnership body;

- Good respectful working relations between the partnership committee or board and any staff appointed;

- Clear division of risks and sharing of any benefits arising from the partnership - eg finance, development opportunities, publicity and public recognition (Vranken 1994).

In practice, the theory of partnership proved rather neater than the reality. A series of documents published by the Poverty 3 central and local teams (Conroy 1994, Bruto da Costa 1994, Estivill et al 1994) also highlight some of the costs, dilemmas, barriers and problems encountered by the Poverty 3 local partnerships:-

- the danger of getting trapped in legal tangles and wrangles over the constitution for partnership bodies;

- the diversity of values, interests and styles between the different bodies represented in the partnership;

- the disparities in power, knowledge, expertise and resources available to the different stakeholders in the partnership;

- the need for training, development and technical advice to enable partners from the voluntary and community sectors to play their full part in the joint venture.

It was also suggested that while the European Commission required an integrated partnership approach by regional and local actors and agencies, it did not involve national governments and did not practise the same level of partnership in its own contribution. While Poverty 3 demonstrated the value of a partnership approach to tackling problems at the local level, and some Member States (eg Ireland) have built on the experience of the programme, more generally there has been only limited progress in disseminating and applying the lessons of Poverty 3.

The LEDA Programme

Evaluation undertaken of the recent LEDA programme (Humphreys 1996), which supported innovative local economic development actions, similarly identified a number of advantages of partnership, arguing that partnership provides a forum for:-

• Consensus, strategy building and co-ordinated action;

• Access to different skills;

• Enhanced outcomes for partners;

• Promotion of innovation;

• Promoting local identity and community and competitiveness.

Partnerships in this research which participated in the LEDA programme include those in Leer, Germany and St Etienne in France.

The evaluation also identified many more problematic issues, ranging from the depth of the contributions made by key partners to the difficulties of evaluating the outcomes and impacts of partnerships, and problems in sustaining them over the long term.

The perspectives of the social partners and other actors

The Economic and Social Committee

ECOSOC has been prominent in advocating a stronger involvement of the social partners and the local authorities in Structural Fund partnerships, and has also suggested that the practice of partnership needs to be extended beyond the economic and social partners, and the other socio-economic agencies and professions, to include direct participation of citizens and their representatives. ECOSOC expressed its commitment to pro-active, pluralistic partnership in its Opinions on Social Exclusion (October 1993) and on the Medium Term Action Programme to Combat Exclusion and Promote Solidarity (December 1993). In these it argues that the European Union can add value to Member States initiatives by, among other things, "creating and supporting networks.... mobilising the relevant players....identifying and promoting good practice, knowledge and expertise....incorporating the fight against social exclusion into the Community's general policies....preventing rather than remedying unemployment and social exclusion."

A distinctive feature of ECOSOC's Opinion was their criticism that the issue of discrimination was not properly addressed: "Negative discrimination, and allied phenomena, such as prejudice, intolerance, extremism and segregation, are structures common to the exclusion faced in many dimensions of social and economic life, by many groups." ECOSOC particularly highlights the needs of women, black and ethnic minority people, disabled people, people with mental illnesses, and religious minorities (European Communities, Economic and Social Committee, 1993a and b).

In its Opinion on the First Cohesion report, ECOSOC draws attention to Member States such as Ireland and Sweden where the social partners and local authorities are actively involved in Monitoring Committees, and expresses the view that vertical and horizontal partnership can be deepened further and made more effective through the greater involvement of local levels and the economic and social partners, helping to bridge the gap between Community structural assistance and citizens at the grassroots. The further development of partnership is, according to ECOSOC, " of far reaching importance for the development of Union citizenship and of democracy and solidarity" (European Communities, Economic and Social Committee 1997).

Trade Unions

The trades unions support the principles of partnership both in the Structural Funds and in relation to anti-poverty policy. They have committed themselves to "un partenariat engagé" and the formation of a European trade union network of struggle against exclusion (Fonteneau, undated). Although the position taken at European level is not always mirrored in practice on the ground, there are numerous examples of trade union activity in local partnerships to combat labour market exclusion and marginalisation, in combination with employers and public and voluntary agencies (Nicaise and Henriques 1995; LASAIRE 1995). The European Trade Union Confederation (ETUC) has argued for the "close consultations" with the social partners "to be defined in more concrete terms" in the application of the Structural Funds (ETUI 1993), and trade union representatives do not feel that partnership in the Structural Funds always meets their expectations. The ETUC now looks towards the new Employment Chapter, and regional employment pacts, as important new contexts for partnership in the employment field.

Business and Employers

UNICE has also indicated its support for partnership, for example in the joint contribution by the social partners in the framework of the European Confidence Pact for Employment. In its position paper on the First Cohesion Report, UNICE argues that the social partners should be involved more closely at all stages of structural policy, from design through to monitoring and evaluation, and supports innovation in the future use of the Structural Funds, in order "to carry out integrated actions targeting economic and social development on the ground" (UNICE, 1997).

The European Declaration of Businesses against Exclusion and the European Business Network for Social Cohesion represent a major initiative by a number of prominent employers to combat exclusion. The Guidelines for Action attached to the Declaration detail specific proposals for businesses to join with other organisations in counteracting exclusion by:-

- promoting integration on the labour market;

- helping to improve vocational training;

- avoiding exclusion within the business, minimising redundancies or providing for appropriate measures where they are inevitable;

- promoting the creation of new jobs and businesses; and

- contributing to social integration in particularly deprived areas and of particularly marginalised groups, including the development of "**priority partnerships** with players from associations, co-operatives and mutual societies, who can offer particularly marginalised persons special assistance with a view to ensuring they can satisfy basic needs....and have access to a job or other activity giving them resources, a regular lifestyle and social recognition" (CEEP 1994; Griffiths 1995; European Business Network for Social Cohesion 1996).

Regional and local authorities

In a similar way to the trades unions and employers, regional and local authorities support the concept of partnership as a means of promoting cohesion but want earlier and more active involvement in the processes both of policy formulation and implementation. The Committee of the Regions (COR) now provides a formal vehicle for regional and local authorities to be consulted and to offer opinions, but their response to the White Paper on European Social Policy suggested that they want partnership to go further than this, emphasising the importance of strengthening the involvement of local and regional local authorities in the ESF monitoring committees. During the European Cohesion Forum in April 1997 numerous local and regional authorities and their national organisations developed this view. For example, the UK Local Government International Bureau states its support for partnership as one of the four main principles governing the operation of the Structural Funds, and calls for regional authorities to have a stronger role alongside governments and the European Commission. The Federation of Swedish County Councils argue that "locally and regionally based partnerships lead to both greater efficiency and the exercise of democratic influence over the Structural Fund system" (European Commission 1997c).

Non-governmental organisations

The European Commission has actively cultivated a collaborative relationship with the voluntary sector and non-governmental organisations in relation to social exclusion. It has offered financial and administrative support towards the setting up of the European Anti-Poverty Network, which is a federal organisation made up of national networks of (largely) voluntary and community organisations in the different Member States. The European Commission has consulted the European Anti Poverty Network on social policy issues, along with other European level organisations like COFACE, the ETUC and UNICE.

The European Social Policy Forum in March 1996 brought together NGOs and the social partners with the European Commission and representatives of the other Institutions. All participants in the Forum recognised the importance of a wide partnership in the struggle against unemployment and exclusion. NGOs demanded more permanent involvement as partners in programmes to combat unemployment and aid the most disadvantaged groups, and wished to see their position in decision making consolidated through more structured partnership with Union Institutions and the social partners (Cousins 1997). These demands reflect the European Anti Poverty Network's concern about the limitations of partnership in practice, and a view that at the moment there are currently few genuine and real partnerships. The NGO sector is willing to play its part but emphasises that effective partnerships need time, commitment and resourcing.

Conclusion

The European Commission appears to reap substantial advantages from drawing many other actors - employers, trade unions, local authorities, non-governmental organisations - into partnership-type relationships. The Commission now collaborates with a range of other bodies with knowledge of national and local conditions and specialist expertise in the fields of local development and regeneration and tackling poverty and exclusion, in the processes of piloting, implementing and evaluating its policies.

Chapter 3

Partnership and the Policy Process: The Experience in Member States

Introduction

This chapter explores the different national contexts of local partnership in the Member States. It outlines the very different patterns and frameworks of social policy and governmental attitudes to public provision, relationships between national, regional and local government and between public authorities and local communities, and different traditions of involvement in social policies on the part of employers, trade unions and voluntary organisations. It shows how these differences have meant that local partnership initiatives to combat social exclusion have developed more or less strongly. Important themes include the extent and manner in which local partnerships have been supported by national or local government policies and programmes; the influence of EU programmes, and the perspectives of the main actors and stakeholders in local partnerships. It thus starts to identify both those factors which support and encourage local partnerships in different policy contexts, and other factors which appear to be barriers to effective local partnership as a method of tackling exclusion, including the nature and degree of involvement of different partners.

An important question is the extent to which there is a general trend towards local partnership as an important component of policies to tackle problems of poverty and exclusion in the different Member States of the EU, including some of those which have joined the EU relatively recently.

The national research reports (Appendix I) each present an analysis of the policy context in which local partnerships have developed in the country concerned. The following country-by-country review draws upon these analyses, and also outlines more briefly important issues in the other five

Member States, drawing on supplementary analysis undertaken for the research programme.

Experience in Member States

Austria

The national policy context

There are two different partnership approaches in Austria: one within the welfare system and one in labour market policy (Kain and Rosian 1996).

In Austria, social policy involves close collaboration between the social partners and the government. Under the Austrian constitution, labour market policy is the responsibility of the Federal government, but the welfare system is primarily the responsibility of the nine federal provinces. In addition, local authorities have certain welfare responsibilities, and the relative roles of provincial and local authorities, and of public, private and voluntary sectors varies from province to province.

Until the mid-1980s, economic growth and full employment were seen as the basis for social protection, but since the decline in economic growth, priorities have changed. The emphasis is now on reducing public expenditure. The 'crisis of the welfare state' is associated with pressures for privatisation and decentralisation, although in practice a pragmatic political compromise tends to favour the development of 'welfare pluralism' - the inclusion of a wider range of bodies in the development and delivery of services and programmes.

Partnership at the local level

In the welfare field, growing demands associated with demographic change and the absence of an integrated approach led in the mid-1970s to the establishment of '*Social Services and Healthcare Districts*', initially in the Tyrol and Vorarlberg. These were intended to expand and network welfare and health provision, and in doing so to include all relevant 'partners' such as the provincial and local authorities, public and private providers and the local community. Partnership approaches are also developing in other welfare fields, such as an initiative in Linz involving the collaboration of different actors around a 'quality of life' workshop.

In the 1980s, a partnership approach also became more prominent in the field of labour market policy, as unemployment, although low by EU standards, rose sharply, with particular problems of long-term and female unemployment. This led to a new emphasis on active labour market policies, including the establishment of **labour foundations,** such as those described in the research in Steyr and Carinthia. These initiatives by the social partners have been established in companies, in industrial sectors, and in regions in response to job losses. They offer a locally-tailored package of measures from career guidance and training to support for new business start-ups. By the end of 1995 there were 43 such foundations, involving the regional social partners, provincial and local governments and the (federal) Employment Service. Other local employment initiatives such as that in Bruck/Mur have been initiated by local authorities.

Socio-economic enterprises are a further instrument of active labour market policy. These are initiatives established for social groups with particular employment problems, such as the long term unemployed or drug addicts. The main promoters are private welfare organisations, but they may also involve the social partners and local communities with public sector funding.

The principal actors

Federal government does not participate directly in the above initiatives at the local level, but is one of the most important interest groups, promoting socio-economic enterprises and labour foundations and exercising a controlling function in labour market policy. Federal government takes the view that provincial governments could be more active in labour market policy both as partners and as founders. **Provincial governments and local authorities** differ greatly in their attitudes. Thus for example the Tyrol provincial government has been particularly active in the promotion of Social Service and Healthcare Districts. Local authorities participate in these both as partners and funders, but tend to be less actively involved in labour foundations. *Other public agencies,* such as the Employment Service, play a significant role in funding both labour foundations and socio-economic enterprises.

Employee representatives are strong supporters of the labour foundations, welcoming their multi-dimensional nature and the inclusion of various interests at the local level. **Employer representatives** are also involved in the labour foundations, and consider that co-operation between the social partners at regional level is useful in gearing policies to specific labour market conditions. They see certain conflicts of interest over the priority they feel is given to employee interests, and the preferential treatment offered to certain firms or sectors.

The voluntary sector in Austria is dominated by several large non-profit organisations which play a leading role in the provision of social services. The attitude of these organisations varies considerably: some welcome the institutionalisation of collaboration, while others fear a loss of their autonomy. Voluntary sector organisations are also often the main promoters of socio-economic enterprises. **Local communities** are mostly only represented in the above arrangements through local authorities or committed individuals: local action groups are rare, and although they are increasing they are seldom formal partners.

Current issues

The development of local partnerships in Austria is still at a very early stage, but is attributable to the financial crisis of the welfare state and to demographic and socio-economic change. The diverse nature of existing forms of collaboration is primarily due to the separation of responsibilities for welfare and labour market policies.

As Austria has been an EU member for only a relatively short time, the development of partnerships as a result of participation in EU programmes (from the European Social Fund to NOW and ADAPT) is only just beginning. However the authorities at national level consider that such programmes are of major importance for the future.

Belgium

The national policy context

According to the national research report (Carton, Delogne, Nicaise and Stengele 1996), social policy issues have entered a complex transitional period in Belgium, between the old 'industrial era' in which a social democratic compromise facilitated inter-class solidarity, to a 'tertiary or ultra-market' society where mass unemployment is destabilising this compromise and creating exclusion.

The period of economic growth, redistributional policies and institutionalised consultation between 1945 and the 1970s has given way to increasing unemployment, declining state revenues and austerity policies in the 1980s and 1990s.

There are also important regional differences in Belgium, with the highest GDP per head in the Brussels region, followed by Flanders, with the lowest level in Wallonia. However, at a more local level there are very run-down areas in even the most prosperous regions, leading to social confrontation and conflict, frequently with an ethnic component.

In this context, the Belgian research suggests, "the welfare state has admitted that its response to complex social problems such as social exclusion is ineffective. Its intervention is too compartmentalised, too unwieldy, and too removed from the marginal groups which it is trying to reach. In addition, faced with budget deficits, the state is reducing its investment in social policy and is seeking to find additional funds from 'partners'" (Carton et al 1996).

Partnership at the local level

The results of this have been apparent in the development of partnership-based initiatives in several policy areas:

- The first issue where a partnership approach was formalised was security. At the beginning of the 1990s the Federal government announced a new policy of 'security contracts' between the federal government and the municipalities in the major conurbations, some linked to poverty issues.

- The subject of education also gave rise to the formulation of various policies (educational priority zones etc) which sought to enhance the standing of the partnership approach amongst various actors (schools, local authorities, associations involved in lifelong education and literacy schemes, health education etc).

- In the area of participation in the labour market, initiatives came from two sources:
  * Initiatives by the social partners to promote inter-sectoral agreements concerning the participation by groups 'at risk'.

  * Initiatives by actors such as local or regional employment agencies and certain voluntary sector organisations.

The principal actors
The municipalities and public services

The municipalities and public services in Belgium are responsible for welfare and are under considerable pressure to develop a partnership approach. They include, first, the Public Centres for Social Welfare (CPAS) which also have a mandate for job creation and labour market reintegration. In Wallonia in 1989, the CPAS were urged to develop greater co-ordination at the local level building stronger networks of cooperation with training organisations, the voluntary sector and industry. This has led to numerous and varied local initiatives (over 100). These are currently proving a key testing ground for a decentralised local approach.

The role of local authorities has been greatly enhanced by new supra-local policies. The Flemish government in 1990 established the *Flemish Fund for the Integration of the Underprivileged* (VFIK), under which 15 municipalities developed multi-dimensional local anti-poverty strategies. The VFIK has now been strengthened and extended as the *Fund to Stimulate Social Action* (SIF).

The social partners

The social partners' traditional importance in Belgium is reflected in the institutionalisation of consultation on labour relations. This has included a new concern with groups at risk in the labour market. In 1989 representatives of employers and employees at national level launched an interesting initiative, in which a special levy of 0.18% of the overall wage bill of companies would be used to provide employment training initiatives for groups at risk. The agreement was renewed in 1991 and the current levy is 0.15%.

There is also increasing trade union involvement in local development initiatives and social enterprises, such as the Initiative Locale pour l'Emploi (ILE), but the association of this development with a shift from public initiative to a more individualised responsibility has led the trade unions to re-emphasise the importance of macro-economic consultation.

The voluntary sector

The voluntary sector has increasingly found itself at the centre of a series of policies and experiments. From a tradition of social and community work, a more multi-dimensional approach has been developed at local level, in active partnership with excluded groups, local authorities, development agencies and so on. In Wallonia, this approach has been led by a platform of major voluntary organisations, called "Solidarity en Plus, Pauvrete en Moins", which has focused attention on the absence of clear state policy priorities. The platform influenced the approach of the Poverty 3 project in Charleroi.

European Union policies

In Belgium the ESF has been of particular importance, providing a framework for synergies and partnership between the CPASs, employment placement services and non-profit organisations in providing integrated routes for employment training. However, experience of ESF initiatives has also served to highlight blockages to more effective partnership caused by the split of responsibilities within the state between the federal level and the regions and between different linguistic regions. ESF schemes have also raised the issue of the position of target groups and the associations working on their behalf in partnerships.

Current issues

The partnership approach to unemployment and social exclusion is currently the subject of considerable debate in Belgium.

At the supra-local level, important new policies and initiatives have been developed, but there is not necessarily adequate coordination between different branches of government, and between federal and regional levels. This is providing new grants and opportunities for actors at the local level, but forcing them 'to co-ordinate what is not co-ordinated elsewhere', and unloading responsibilities to the local level without a clear management framework. The form of this 'local unloading' in Belgium raises particular questions concerning a 'democratic deficit', in that collective local action is developing, but with a lack of involvement of the target/excluded groups themselves.

Partnership in Belgium was seen therefore as cooperation between unequal partners: "although all the relevant parties at the local level may be or become involved in the collective action, their individual contributions in terms of role, power and resources are not equal". Moreover, the context of partnership remains open to question: "it is necessary to ask whether and to what extent we are talking about an increase in social provision, a redistribution of services, or merely a process of decentralisation" (Carton et al, 15, 17).

Finland

The national policy context

Until recently there has been little discussion in Finland on the subject of partnership as a socio-political means of combating unemployment and social exclusion. This is because the role of the public sector has long been predominant in the area of welfare. Universal social policy according to the lines of the Scandinavian welfare state model has been the guiding principle behind government policies, and this objective has been realised through the channelling of resources into a structural social policy, in which the role of the public sector has been of supreme importance in both the social security and public service areas (Heikkila and Kautto 1996).

However during the economic recession of the 1990s the unemployment rate in Finland rose from 3% to almost 18%, and is currently still over 15%. The state has rapidly moved into debt, and the increase in public expenditure has forced governments into making cuts. The organisation of welfare is now being reshaped while unemployment has grown alarmingly with the dangers of exclusion that go with it.

Despite these economic difficulties, at the time of the research partnership had not been considered as a new policy option. Interviews with important decision makers at national level showed that there was still wide support to tackle social problems with the measures presently in place. It can be argued that exclusion in Finland has not, for the present, assumed such drastic proportions that it calls the legitimacy of the present system into question. Poverty has been kept at bay, to the extent that the question of exclusion has not yet entered the vocabulary of politicians, nor has there been any crucial debate on the subject.

Nevertheless, the Finnish research provides evidence of co-operation relevant to the notion of partnership at both national and local level. Developments since the national research was undertaken show a growing interest in the partnership approach in Finland.

The principal actors

At **national level**, a form of partnership can be identified in the so-called tripartite system, in which negotiations concerning pay, working conditions and related issues are conducted by government with the central organisations of the social partners (employers and employees). At **local level**, the main roles are played by the municipalities and voluntary organisations. One important instrument in maintaining this relationship is a joint body of the state and voluntary organisations, the *Finnish Slot Machine Association*, which finances projects at the grassroots and local level. Partnership-type initiatives at local level are emerging as a consequence of the restructuring of service delivery. The importance of local authorities is likely to grow due to the decentralisation of administration, reforms in the system of state subsidies, and encouragement of citizen participation.

Current issues

Since Finland has only been a member of the EU since January 1995, it is difficult at this stage to assess the influence of the Union in promoting partnership. Compared to the total social budget, the resources available from the EU are fairly scanty. Nevertheless, great interest is now discernible in such new sources of funding, and in the modes of operation demanded by them.

Very recently, a Ministry of Labour committee has made new proposals for local employment initiatives, under the title, 'The Finnish model of local initiative and partnership', in response to the European Commission's initiative on regional employment pacts. A three year programme is proposed, establishing 20 local partnerships across Finland, under the co-ordination of a 'partnership executive group' in the Ministry. These would be based on collaboration between the state and the municipalities, with greater space allocated for the third sector in job creation. Partnership has also been a theme in discussion on the social responsibility of business by the Finnish President.

There are therefore some indications that in the new context of EU membership, local partnerships may become a more visible element in the Finnish response to unemployment and exclusion.

France

The national policy context
In France, partnership represents a shift from the centralist tradition of state policy and the clear division between the public and private sectors (Le Gales and Loncle 1997).

From 1945 until the mid-1970s, the dirigiste, centralised French state played a dominant role in reconstruction, economic planning and social and urban policy. The all-pervading influence of the state had its counterpoints in a disregard for local authorities and the voluntary sector and the relative weakness of trade unions and employer organisations. This "inevitably precluded any discourse or practices which were closely or remotely akin to partnership" (Le Gales and Loncle, 2). The fruits of economic growth and the institutionalisation of the welfare state raised hopes of a permanent eradication of poverty.

In the more recent period however a number of factors have combined to change this position, and to lead to the development of collaboration between public and private organisations in the area of economic development, and between different public sector bodies in the area of social policy. The traditional instruments used by the state have been found wanting: they have not been so effective, they have lacked legitimacy, and resources have become increasingly scarce. Consequently forms of partnership have emerged to complement or replace state or public action, often as part of a neo-liberal approach which seeks to reduce the role of the state and allow private actors to exert some control over state policies and introduce a more market oriented system.

Partnership at the local level
From the 1970s several developments converged to question the centralised approach to public policy: the crisis in the welfare state, an urban crisis, and decentralisation policies. The 'discovery' of 'new poverty', especially in urban areas, was linked to periodic riots in the 1980s and 1990s. In the early 1980s, the state decentralised several areas of responsibility to local government and

local agencies, but while this increased local autonomy it also produced a major fragmentation of public intervention and power struggles between public authorities at various levels. The partnership approach appeared as one way of re-establishing a consistency of intervention by public bodies to combat social exclusion.

This is apparent in the evolution of urban and other policies. The *Habitat et Vie Sociale* initiative in the 1970s first promoted collaboration between state and local officials and professionals. The *Development Social des Quartiers* programme of the early 1980s transferred much greater power to local authorities and elected representatives and stimulated a multitude of innovative, horizontal and 'partnership-type' initiatives. The *Contrat de Ville* programme of the late 1980s promoted closer collaboration between the regional tier of the state and local authorities within the framework of national social policy, through a series of local 'contracts' between the two partners. The recent *Urban Renewal Pact* gives greater emphasis to economic development and employment, but despite a language of partnership represents a move back towards central control.

Other important policies which have instituted a more collaborative approach to urban policy include the Zones d'Education Prioritaire, the Operations Programmeés d'Ete, the Conseils Communaux de Prevention de la Délinquance, and more recently, the Local Commissions for Employment Initiatives and urban reconstruction agreements between the state, local authorities and major private companies. In addition to such formal partnership or contract arrangements, there are of course many more informal networks in the urban and social policy fields.

The principal actors
The partnership approach in France has largely involved three sectors: the public and quasi-public sector, the voluntary sector and the social partners, with most of the funding coming from the public sector, including the EU.

The public sector. The main players in partnership-type structures come from the public sector, but these are very varied. They include:-

• State ministries and agencies including the regional prefectures;

• Local and regional authorities;

- Elected representatives, national and regional civil servants and other officials.

Consequently public sector participation in partnership arrangements can be subject to complex procedures, and to conflict and rivalry between different parts of the public sector.

Semi-public organisations play a key role, for example the social security offices and the offices responsible for public housing.

The voluntary sector is extremely diverse. At the national level large federations of associations, including bodies concerned with the fight against poverty and exclusion, have been concerned to try to widen the scope of partnership by positioning the voluntary sector 'between government and the market'. At the local, level local associations are frequently involved in partnership-type initiatives, but their representativeness has been questioned.

The involvement of the **social partners** has been more limited but there are several examples of innovative experiments at the local level. While it is still an exception for employer organisations to be involved in partnerships established to combat social exclusion, in some cases foundations such as the Fondation Agir play an important intermediary role. The participation of trade unions is extremely localised. Some unions have given priority to the struggle against exclusion and in some places there have been campaigns which have brought the trade unions together with other sympathetic partners, such as the mutual banking networks.

European Union programmes, such as LEDA, LEADER and the Poverty programmes have played a significant role in France in encouraging a broad partnership approach and also in promoting transnational exchange.

Germany

The national policy context

In Germany the concept of local partnership adopted for this research project is relatively little known, although great importance is attached to the concept of partnership in a wider sense (Birkholzer and Lorenz 1996).

Until the reunification of the two German states in 1990 there were two different starting situations for partnership to promote social cohesion in Germany. The original Federal Republic of Germany was the classic example of social partnership in Europe, with the postwar consensus around the concept of a social market economy providing the basis for collaboration between employers and trade unions at national, regional and plant level. Bodies responsible for unemployment insurance, social security and vocational training were characterised by tripartite partnership between the social partners and government. However with the slowdown of economic growth in the 1970s and 1980s this consensus started to be eroded. A debate on the modernisation of the welfare state has led to widely differing views as to whether it is being concerted and rebuilt (the federal government and employers), or dismantled (trade unions, many municipalities and districts, voluntary sector).

In the former GDR the term partnership was not used as such, but there were forms of collaboration, for example between companies and internal company trade unions, and young people and the elderly, which promoted social cohesion.

Since the mid 1970s problems of unemployment and social exclusion have increased in Germany, with considerable debate about the relevance of the term 'new poverty'. Reunification added an 'east-west' dimension to the previous duality between 'rich south' and 'poor north'. Increasing structural economic and social crisis has brought official unemployment levels of 9-11%, an income poverty level of about 10%, and major problems of substandard housing and inadequate social services especially in the east. The concentration of social exclusion in certain areas, including both urban neighbourhoods and rural areas means that unemployment and exclusion pose serious problems for specific social groups but also particular localities.

Partnership at the local level

It is these developing urban and rural crises that have led to the beginnings of specifically local partnerships of the kind studied in this research. In such 'crisis regions', according to the German research study, local initiative is gaining ground "because neither the private sector - through investment - nor the public sector - through intervention - are achieving a decisive or comprehensive turnaround" (Birkholzer and Lorenz, 6). The research study identifies a number of such grassroots initiatives, for example in Wedding in Berlin and in the village of Wulkow in Brandenburg. However there are as yet no major regional or national programmes to foster the bottom up initiatives which are now emerging, and which therefore remain largely informal. They do not generally describe themselves as partnerships.

The principal actors

European Union policies

A few local partnerships of the type defined in this research have been established on the basis of EU programmes such as those in Friedrichshain, Berlin, and Leer funded by the Poverty 3, LEADER and LEDA programmes. However, the wider influence of these has been limited, and most local partnerships currently in existence have been the result of initiatives by local authorities, employees and a range of local groups.

The public sector

Those public sector actors who have initiated partnerships are frequently convinced of the effectiveness of the partnership approach. However, others who have been involved as more passive representatives tend to be more cautious.

The social partners

In the case of both employers and trade unions, involvement in local partnerships by employers organisations or trade unions is limited. However, there is greater involvement and support by individual businesses, especially smaller businesses, social enterprises and farmers in rural areas; and by local trade unionists or groups of workers.

The voluntary sector

Although in many cases it is voluntary organisations which have initiated local partnership activity, those involved are often sceptical about the long term viability of the approach, because they feel they cannot rely on the continuing loyalty of organisations in the public and private sectors, especially the large organisations.

Women and ethnic minorities

Women play a leading role in many of the local partnerships studied in the German research, but the organisations of ethnic minorities are barely represented in them. There appears to be some involvement of economic immigrants at a local level, who have become more socially integrated into local communities, but not of political asylum seekers and refugees.

Current issues

In Germany, local partnerships concerned with unemployment and social exclusion remain largely dependent on grassroots initiative. They are not generally supported by Federal or regional programmes, and the influence of EU policies has been limited.

National and regional initiatives are much more important in the public perception. These include the Federal government's "Action Programme for Investment and Jobs" and the "Alliance for Jobs" between employer and employee organisations. However it may be important to note that the local level is becoming increasingly prominent in this context: local or regional alliances for jobs have now been proposed or set in train in many localities.

Greece

The national policy context

The Greek research report notes that the development of partnerships to tackle social exclusion is predicated both on the recognition of such problems and on a policy context favourable to the involvement of leading actors. In postwar Greece, under the dictatorial regime, the state controlled every aspect of life, and did not allow the development of independent social organisations such as trade unions, cooperatives and other associations. The economic system which developed was based on state intervention and assistance. Consequently, prior to the establishment of parliamentary democracy in 1974, none of the conditions for the development of a partnership approach to social exclusion existed (Robolis, Papadogamvros, Dimoulas and Sidira 1996).

After 1974, free expression was allowed together with the basic rights of assembly and association. By the 1980s, the paternalistic character of state politics began to diminish and a rudimentary form of state corporatism emerged, with a gradual movement towards a pluralistic process for articulating interests, support for local government and dialogue with the voluntary sector. However the development of social welfare policies has tended to be piecemeal and unco-ordinated, and based not on associative principles but on a traditional model of state support.

At just under half the average of all EU countries, per capita GNP in Greece is lower than that of any other Member State. Owing to improvements in living standards and welfare provision social exclusion has not been recognised as a problem until the last decade, when there has been a protracted economic crisis, restrictive income and financial policies and a downturn in the employment market. At the same time, Greece has been transformed from a country of emigration to one of immigration, resulting in some new problems of social exclusion.

Partnership at the local level

Partnerships at the local level for combating problems associated with social exclusion are extremely limited, due to the centralised nature of the Greek state and the very limited tradition of independent action on the part of local government and the voluntary sector. Those which exist have usually been set up under EU programmes such as the initiatives in Perama with their origins in the Poverty 3 programme or those for women in West Attica supported by the NOW Community Initiative. Most have been concerned with the implementation of training programmes in urban areas.

The main actors

Central government.

National policies in Greece are based on traditional corporatist welfare practices deeply influenced by clientilistic relations. State welfare is limited, inadequate and unco-ordinated, and governed by inflexible administrative and bureaucratic procedures. Thus while over the last few years elements of a partnership approach have appeared, there is as yet no overall commitment to a partnership approach by central government.

Local authorities.

The limited extent to which local government has developed autonomy and financial independence in Greece has also influenced the lack of partnerships at local level. Local government still tends to play the role of intermediary for central government, and has only recently begun to develop a more innovative approach. However in the last decade new regional and local institutions have been set up, offering local government the possibility of a more developmental role in both local economic development and social assistance and welfare.

State and quasi-state bodies.

Quasi-state bodies such as the National Manpower Employment Service (OAED) play an important role in implementing social policy in Greece. They are managed by a combination of government and corporatist control. They tend to operate in a detached and paternalistic manner, although there are some signs of a more consultative approach .

The social partners.

Industrial development in Greece is limited, with the majority of businesses being SMEs which have grown up against a background of state protectionism and a limited market. Many businesses are facing serious economic and competitiveness problems which means that in most cases they are not active in local partnerships.

Until 1982 the trade unions were concerned mainly with recognition of their legal status and obtaining civil and trade union freedoms. In recent years they have begun to develop closer collaboration with other actors, such as local government, in relation to problems of social exclusion. The General Confederation of Greek Workers and the major employers associations have recently moved to set up joint committees on specific problems, including long-term unemployment and employment support, involving bilateral and trilateral collaboration between the social partners and with government.

The voluntary sector
The voluntary sector is only weakly developed in Greece, and is largely limited to pressure group activities.

Communities and community organisations
Traditionally in Greece the church, the family and neighbours have played an important part in maintaining social cohesion. The church cooperates closely with the state in welfare provision, and family and kinship networks are at the heart of social life, but for different reasons these have not contributed to the development of partnership in the sense defined in this research.

The European Union
Several EU programmes, including Poverty 3, NOW and HORIZON have been important in promoting the concept of local partnership in the very specific Greek context, but the development of partnerships associated with these and other programmes has met with great difficulties. The Poverty 3 programme had to contend with a lack of definition of problems of poverty and exclusion, and conservative attitudes towards the measures required. Those partnerships that were developed were seen as foreign and imposed from the top down. Nonetheless, the philosophy of these programmes has had a definite influence, especially perhaps in local government, leading to proposals to create partnerships to implement a number of sub-programmes of the Operational Programme on Social Exclusion under the second Community Support Framework.

Ireland

The national policy context
Ireland has experienced a major transformation of its economy and society since the early 1960s. The state adopted a strategy of economic development based on foreign industrial investment which resulted in record levels of industrial growth. Accompanying this economic strategy has been a rapid expansion of the welfare state, with an increase in employment in the public and semi-state sectors and expansion of education and welfare services including income support, health and housing. A feature of government strategy has been a

succession of tripartite agreements with employers and trade unions in the 1980s and 1990s (Walsh, Craig and McCafferty 1997).

The weakness in this performance however has been the high and persistent level of unemployment (13%) and particularly of long-term unemployment, among less skilled workers in both the urban and rural sectors. Government temporary employment initiatives targeted at the unemployed have had only limited success. Poverty levels have increased over the period from the mid-1970s to the mid-1990s, with 15% of the population classified as 'consistently poor'. The high incidence of poverty and social exclusion is compounded by gender and other inequalities, segregation in the housing market, differential access to services and conditions of dependency and powerlessness.

Social partnership between sectoral interests is at the core of public policy in Ireland, and more recently NGOs have been included in this framework for the first time. The deepening and widening of social partnership to address the persistent problems of unemployment and poverty has provided the key context for the emergence of local partnerships as promoters of social inclusion. At the same time, three other factors have been important: an emphasis on local economic development as part of a strengthening of the local dimension in public administration; a reassessment of traditional welfare-based policies to tackle social exclusion, leading to the development of multi-sectoral strategies targeted at specific areas of disadvantage with a more active approach; and official support for community development as a means of empowering disadvantaged groups and communities.

Partnership at the local level
Following a number of innovative and pilot local partnership programmes from the mid 1980s onward, the government has made partnership-led local development an integral component of economic and social policy, with strong political and administrative leadership from the Department of the Taoiseach. Numerous new structures have been set up at local level under this policy framework, which offer different approaches to local partnership in terms of their structure, remit and area of operation. These include:

- 70 local development partnerships

- 35 local enterprise boards

- 100+ local development organisations

- 70 community development projects

- 4 urban renewal partnerships.

EU policies, funding and transnational networks have had a major influence on the development of local partnership in Ireland, with a particular feature of the Irish experience being the way in which many local partnerships have created synergy between European and national resources.

The principal actors

Central government

Central government has played a crucial role in promoting local partnerships as a policy instrument, and its assessment of them is overwhelmingly positive. The partnership principle is regarded as a means of mobilising local interests in pursuit of local needs, and the emphasis on the local is seen as a complement to economic and social development at the national level. While some in central government see partnership in terms of a loose alliance of local interests, others regard local partnerships as reflecting the social partnership structures at national level between government, employers and trade unions, and increasingly the NGO sector.

Other public agencies

In the Irish context these include the economic development, health and education authorities, local government, policy advice agencies such as the Combat Poverty Agency and semi-independent administrative bodies including Area Development Management Ltd which funds and supports local partnerships. A much stronger role in local partnerships is played by central government agencies at the regional level than by local government, which has little responsibility for social and economic development and is often only marginally involved. Despite inevitable differences of perspective, most of these bodies recognise the value of local partnerships in mobilising efforts and promoting an integrated approach to unemployment and social exclusion, with the specific value of involving excluded groups in a way which helps to balance traditional power relations.

Employers and trade unions

Employers and trade unions contribute to local partnership both at the macro level and through participation in individual local partnerships. They have been involved in establishing, monitoring and guiding programmes which support local partnerships. Employers' main interest in partnerships is their capacity to promote enterprise and create jobs. They are involved directly in local partnerships both individually and through forums such as the Enterprise Trust which supports local enterprise development. For the trade unions, the emphasis is on the role of partnerships in combating long term unemployment. The network of local centres for the unemployed also form a link between the trade union movement and local partnerships.

The social partners regard local partnership as having many advantages, including its ability to cut through state bureaucracy, but are more critical in their judgements than other interests. with concerns about the costs of partnerships, their reliance on public funding and the new bureaucracy which they may involve.

Community and voluntary groups

A defining feature of local partnerships in Ireland is the involvement of local community interests in their management and operation. The input of the community sector occurs at three levels:

- involvement in national policy making through various national network organisations such as those for women, the unemployed, and for travellers.

- support for the activities of local partnerships by national network associations.

- the participation of local community groups in local partnerships, where the sector is guaranteed membership of boards and committees.

Community and voluntary groups view partnerships as a useful mechanism for accessing resources, improving the provision of public services, generating economic development, and for dialogue with other interests. But they are conscious of the demands it places on the sector, and voice a concern about the representation of more minority interests.

Research and other technical consultants

These organisations are seen by the Irish research study as having a distinctive role and voice, particularly related to programme and project support and evaluation, and the provision of education and training programmes. These organisations generally acknowledge the merits of the partnership approach, while cautioning against a straitjacket application of it. They emphasise issues such as the importance of the transfer of good practice between local partnerships, and vertical co-ordination between national, county/urban and neighbourhood levels.

Current issues

Among the important issues concerning local partnership in Ireland are the questions concerning the role of local authorities and elected representatives, and the 1997 initiative by the Irish government to implement a national anti-poverty strategy.

Portugal

The national policy context

In Portugal, the principle of partnership has two distinct meanings. *Parceria* (informal partnership) refers to traditions and practices of social collaboration and solidarity among individuals with shared interest, with deep historical roots. *Partenariado* (formal partnership) on the other hand, has only emerged recently in Portugal, mainly as a result of European Union programmes, and is consequently often perceived in terms of transnational collaboration among 'partners' in various Member States, rather than among local interests (Rodrigues, Stoer and Vaz 1996).

During the 1960s and 1970s, the tradition of *parceria* was an important component of the community development movement which is one of the important antecedents of contemporary partnership. The community development approach rejected both the corporatist tradition of the authoritarian centralist period, and a narrowly economic approach to development. Instead it promoted a concept of multidisciplinary activity, based in local initiatives which sought to be catalysts of change, with participation and co-operation central to their philosophy, and bringing together local populations and public authorities.

During the 1980s however, particularly with Portugal's accession to the EU in 1986, the formal conception of partnership has become increasingly hegemonic, with 'partnership' being a requirement for participation in EU programmes and becoming a key term in official economic and social policies. In the late 1980s and early 1990s, a further dimension has been a number of 'partnership' agreements between the social partners concerning issues such as incomes and prices, health and safety and vocational training.

Portugal remains one of the least industrialised countries in Europe, and poverty affects 25 - 30% of the population, with profound inequalities between social groups and regions. The fact that 60% of the unemployed receive no unemployment benefit indicates the limited nature of welfare provision in Portugal. It was not until the early 1970s that the state began to serve as a central provider of welfare, with the objective of establishing a universal welfare system. In practice, however, welfare has remained based on the twin pillars of "co-operative companionship" between the state and the non-profit making private sector, while in the 1980s there has been a trend towards some restriction of social rights and the commercialisation of welfare.

Local partnership
The forms of local partnership which exist in Portugal are varied. In the more formal partnerships (the partnership, which was supported by the Poverty 3 Programme in Porto is a good example) the most active partners are the central, regional and local public authorities. In some of the partnerships, such as the IN LOCO local development initiative in southern Portugal and ARCIL in the centre of the country, which is concerned with the needs of those with disabilities, informal networks of collaboration among voluntary and community organisations are more important.

The main actors
Government in Portugal has developed a number of programmes in which partnership plays an important role. In 1990 a national anti-poverty programme was launched, drawing on the EU Poverty 3 programme, under which some 100 local partnership projects were to be developed. In 1991, a new Directorate General of Social Action was created, embodying a partnership culture and complementarity between public and private organisations. In 1993, a Special Rehousing Programme made explicit reference to the need for local initiatives to be based on collaboration both between central and local public authorities and also other interests. The Second Community Support Framework is also important in its explicit reference to various partners' contributions.

Employers organisations
Employers organisations are also influenced by the promotion of partnership by the EU, and have shown considerable interest in initiatives such as Europartenariat, although the tendency is to perceive partnership in terms of exchange between economic partners.

The trade unions
The trade unions have also been affected by the European Union, especially by the implications of the 'European social dimension', and this has promoted a greater concern for collaboration with other interests in the fields of human and social rights, and work issues such as job creation and training in areas and sectors of high unemployment.

Current issues

The Portuguese research suggests that there is considerable agreement among the main actors on a number of issues about partnership. These include, first, the fact that partnership takes time to develop and create a partnership culture. Secondly, that it brings certain advantages, including the sharing of resources and knowledge to produce more viable projects, creating local trust and collaboration and the potential to influence national policies. Thirdly however, there is agreement on some disadvantages, notably the costs of partnership working, the strings attached to external aid and the danger of a retreat by the state in the sphere of social policy. A key issue now is seen to be the need to articulate the more formal, 'European' concept of *partenariado* with the locally-rooted traditions of *parceria*.

Spain

The national policy context

The Spanish research report is at pains to point out that, in Spain, partnership is not a clear-cut concept but is open to different interpretations. It is difficult to draw a line between dialogue, co-operation, participation and partnership, and between more and less formalised partnership approaches (Estivill and Martinez 1996).

Nonetheless, the research suggests the growing importance of local partnership in Spain, in part as a result of the influence of EU membership, but also as a result of factors such as the institutional structure of government; the changing relationship between the public and private sectors; an emerging debate about the relationship between economic and social issues; increasing recognition of problems of poverty and exclusion, and the development of new strategies against poverty.

The Spanish state is organised territorially at four levels: central administration; 17 Autonomous Communities, such as the Basque country or Catalonia; 54 Provinces; and local authorities. In the social policy field, there is an extremely complex distribution of competencies, both between these four levels and in public/private sector terms. This leads to overlapping, gaps in provision, and, especially in a context of shortage of money, to 'co-ordination' and 'consultation' becoming two of the most frequently used words of the 1990s.

The respective roles of the public and private sectors in social provision have been the subject of prolonged debate. At the end of the Franco period, over 60% of social services were privately provided, but criticisms of private provision led to growing support for public intervention. However in the 1980s the picture changed. The consequences of economic crisis were making themselves felt, so that a limited expansion of public funding had to cope with increasing needs and demands, and the bureaucratic limitations of public provision were also being exposed. 'Market' criteria of productivity and efficiency became increasingly important, with a growing presence of both for-profit providers and the voluntary sector, so that 'partnership' within a mixed market was seen as preferable to either public sector hegemony or excessive profit-taking.

The partnership approach to problems of social exclusion involves an integration of economic and social factors. In Spain, there have been two dominant views on this issue. The first has stressed the importance of market forces, regarding social issues as secondary. The second has seen economic development and competitiveness as the primary issue, but in the context of a social pact which assigns and redistributes resources. These have been the viewpoints of employers. On the other hand, the social welfare viewpoint has been that economic decisions should be made from a fundamental belief in people's welfare. However, recent years have seen a greater rapprochement between these two positions, with economic actors beginning to accept social responsibilities and those responsible for welfare setting up commercial activities.

These changes in the policy context have been influenced by a new awareness of problems of poverty and exclusion in the 1980s. Unemployment in Spain is now at one of the highest levels in the European Union, especially for older and younger workers, with particular problems of long term unemployment and precarious employment. The social protection system does not fully address such problems, with over half of all unemployed people receiving no unemployment compensation, and a social security system which tends to exacerbate inequality.

Partnership at the local level

The much higher visibility of poverty has however led to important policy developments, especially in the field of minimum income. A minimum income policy pioneered in the Basque country in 1989 has spread across the whole of Spain, and is now the main component of public action aimed at combating the most extreme forms of poverty and exclusion. This has advanced partnership relationships in various ways: between regional, provincial and local administrations; and with economic and social interests. In some regions, such as the Basque country and Catalonia, minimum income policies have led to the development of integrated, 'global' plans to combat poverty and exclusion, drawing particularly on principles from the EU's Poverty 3 programme.

The main actors

The public sector

The public administration has become more open to partnership processes during the 1990s, both between different territorial levels of the state, and horizontally among different areas at a given administrative level, and involving other players.

Collective, intermediary and voluntary organisations

A range of these organisations are important in partnership relationships at different levels. Intermediate associations - foundations, associations, co-operatives - have become increasingly well established in the delivery of social services. Some of the large voluntary organisations enjoy high visibility and representation at state level. Collective initiatives may be on a geographical basis, related to a specific social group, or issue-based. Such initiatives are often transitory, but can also form effective coalitions at local, regional, and state level, and have a considerable impact as advocates for the demands of excluded groups.

Trade unions

Trade unions have returned to an involvement in social affairs during the 1980s, for example in the campaign for minimum pay, and have begun to concern themselves increasingly with the situation of excluded groups, especially over issues such as training, integration and care, and in local and regional projects, although such an involvement poses difficult issues for them.

Employers

In Spain it is necessary to draw a distinction between the employers' associations and individual companies. While the former have only a minimal interest in exclusion, at regional and local level there is some employer participation in initiatives, such as training and integration, which go beyond companies' own objectives. For example, voluntary organisations of retired and working entrepreneurs contribute their know-how to the establishment of companies and social projects; and some multinationals make efforts to recruit individuals who have been excluded. They also involve themselves in community development projects.

Current issues

The context in Spain is now more open to ideas of partnership. The players are increasingly prepared to listen to one another, and to sit round a table negotiating, agreeing and developing actions against exclusion. A large number of partnership-type initiatives are now springing up, but a high proportion of them fall by the wayside.

United Kingdom

The national policy context

In the UK the emergence of a local partnership approach to problems of social exclusion has been associated with several linked factors: the emergence of partnership as a perceived solution to a wide range of complex and intractable public policy problems; the increasing role in public policy of business, market models and managerial methods; an emphasis on localised responsibility for policy implementation; and the growth of poverty and exclusion (Geddes and Benington 1996).

The UK has experienced a more rapid increase in social inequality and poverty than any other EU member state, both as a result of exclusion from employment and growing differentials in income from paid employment. The growth of poverty and exclusion is now widely recognised to be damaging to social cohesion and also to economic competitiveness. The geographical concentration of poverty has also increased in recent years, confirming the need for spatially targeted, multi-dimensional and multi-agency responses.

Local partnerships

Local partnerships are regarded as an important element in the policy response to problems of poverty and exclusion in the UK, supported by government programmes such as City Challenge and the Single Regeneration Budget, and endorsed across the political spectrum. The most direct impetus behind the growth of local partnership has been the fact that increasingly both UK government and EU funding programmes have required a strong partnership framework as a precondition for access to funding. Beneath this specific pressure, the research suggests that the emergence of the local partnership approach reflects a number of linked factors:

•   the perceived limitations of traditional public services, the consequent reduction in the resources for public provision over the past fifteen years, and the need for coordination among a growing number of newly created state and quasi-state agencies;

•   as the role of local authorities as service providers has been eroded, many have developed civic leadership roles which emphasise a partnership approach;

- the emergence of grassroots and community self-help initiatives in some areas;

- the increasingly important role of voluntary agencies in service provision;

- the encouragement by government of business involvement in local regeneration projects.

The main actors

Local partnerships in the UK typically include partners from the public, private, voluntary and community sectors, but trade unions are less frequently involved. The lead role is most frequently taken by public or quasi-public agencies. While some local partnerships in the UK involve only informal collaboration among local actors, many, especially those supported by major funding programmes, involve formal organisational structures, strategies and processes distinct from those of partner agencies. However local partnership is less strongly developed in rural areas, partly because of the emphasis in the UK on problems of urban regeneration.

Government

At national government level, a partnership approach is endorsed by all the main political parties and is strongly promoted in many government programmes. Local government has become increasingly supportive of a partnership approach, while lobbying for a greater recognition of issues such as local democratic accountability which are raised by partnerships. Local quasi-governmental agencies such as Training and Enterprise Councils (LECs in Scotland) play an important role in many local regeneration partnerships.

Employer

Employer participation in local partnerships has been strongly advocated by recent governments, although in practice employer involvement at the local level varies widely from the largely symbolic to a much more substantial stake, especially where partnerships are delivery mechanisms for major regeneration projects.

Trade union

Trade union participation in local partnerships is relatively limited in the UK.

The voluntary sector

The voluntary sector, including both large national and small local voluntary organisations, is making a growing contribution to local partnership activity, supported by the National Council for Voluntary Organisations. The involvement of the *local community and community organisations* is seen as a key element of the local partnership approach in the UK. Organisations representing the community sector have welcomed this but have called for further steps to support the fuller involvement of community representatives.

Current issues

Although local partnership is strongly established in the UK, the review of the perspectives of partners and policymakers revealed several important issues. Many policymakers suspect that partnership is frequently only skin-deep, especially where it reflects an element of compulsion rather than a willing commitment by some partners. It is often not clear how far the activities of different partners are consistent in practice with a partnership's objectives. There are concerns about the costs of partnership working, and the need for effective monitoring of the specific contribution of partnership to policy outcomes. Finally, the extent to which local regeneration partnerships give priority to problems of poverty and exclusion can be an issue.

The other Member States

In **Denmark** there is a long tradition of partnership at the national level between the social partners: it may be said that a national contract between the organisations of the employers and the employees laid the basis of the Danish welfare state. Denmark also has strong traditions of local organisation and of decentralisation, and these have been important factors in the establishment of local partnership-type initiatives, many of which include grassroots organisations. Since the late 1980s there has been rising concern among policymakers about the problem of social exclusion, and national policies and programmes have been introduced promoting local partnerships. The EU Poverty 3 programme has also been an important influence.

The **Italian** context for local partnerships is complex because of the fact that the welfare system is markedly fragmented on a regional basis. However a consistent trend is one of pressure on state welfare provision, driven by fiscal constraints, which threatens the search for a more adequate response to problems of exclusion. As a consequence, while formal local partnerships are not a major feature, there are a variety of partnership type relationships between the public sector and other actors (the private sector, charities, trade unions, cooperatives, associations).

Luxembourg, with its high standard of living and small population, does not face the same problems of social exclusion as other European countries. Moreover, because of the small size of the country, social policies operate primarily at the national level, not on an area basis. Nonetheless, some initiatives show that collaboration between different partners, in urban renewal for example and especially between public and voluntary organisations, has met with some success in those instances where it has been tried.

In the **Netherlands** the primary policy framework concerned with social exclusion is the national Social Renewal policy which is implemented through a system of global contracts with the municipalities. Currently steps are being taken to introduce greater co-ordination in tackling social exclusion within national government. The intention is that this will provide a basis for a more integrated local approach to social exclusion, and for co-operation between public services, welfare and voluntary organisations and local employers. However there are few formal local partnerships on the lines of the definition adopted in this research.

Swedish policies to combat social exclusion are closely tied to the Swedish welfare state, which is based on principles of universalism, solidarity and the provision of income-related, non-means tested benefits. The constitution establishes that public authorities, at central and local level, have the overall responsibility for welfare. However, over the past decade the welfare state has come under pressure for various reasons: slower economic growth and increasing demands on public services. The 1990s recession intensified these problems and brought a major increase in unemployment and marginalisation. In this context, new forms of welfare provision involving private and voluntary providers have been investigated. This has led to increased collaboration at local level between different agencies, which may be a precursor of more formal partnerships

Conclusion

The picture which emerges across the Member States is clearly one of considerable diversity. Nonetheless a number of linked factors are frequently associated with the development of a local partnership approach to problems of poverty and exclusion. These include:

- Declining or low rates of economic growth, and persistent economic crisis;

- The growth of 'new', widespread, structural unemployment and poverty and problems of exclusion, with a marked urban and regional dimension;

- A fiscal crisis of the welfare state, linked to criticisms of state services and of over-centralisation;

- Moves towards **decentralisation** of functions within the state to regional and local authorities, and a *de-centering* of the state, with the development of a mixed market in social provision among public, private and not-for-profit providers. In some Southern European countries, these trends have coincided with processes of **democratisation** in the transition from previously authoritarian regimes.

- The nature of the relationships between government, employers and trade unions concerning economic and social policy;

- National (or regional) government programmes promoting and supporting local partnerships;

- The influence of EU policies and programmes.

The manner and the extent to which these trends have occurred in different countries, and the points in time at which they have become important, appear to have had an important influence on the extent to which a local partnership approach has been adopted.

Perhaps the most important conclusion to be drawn from this chapter concerns the role of **national and regional government programmes** which encourage (or in some cases require) and fund local partnerships. There are several kinds of policies and programmes which play this role.

- National programmes to support **integrated local development and regeneration**, in both **urban and rural** contexts, have been a driving force in the establishment of local partnerships in a number of countries, including the United Kingdom, Ireland, France and the Netherlands. In some countries, programmes of this type are the responsibility of the regional authorities, as in the case of the Flemish Funds for the Integration of the Underprivileged, and the Funds to Combat Social Exclusion in the Walloon region of Belgium. Not all of these programmes, however, embody a specific commitment to a formal local partnership approach. There are also considerable differences in the priority given to combating poverty and social exclusion within such programmes.

- National programmes supporting **social development or local community development**, as in the Community Development Programme in Ireland and the Social Development Programme in Denmark, can be particularly important in supporting local partnerships which are specifically focused on deprived communities and problems of poverty and social exclusion.

- Programmes promoting **local economic development and local labour market** initiatives, such as the Local Enterprise Programme in Ireland and the Labour Foundations in Austria are a third type of national programme which support local partnerships.

It is clear from the research that the presence or absence of such policies is, not surprisingly, one of the crucial factors influencing the extent to which local partnerships have emerged, and the orientation of such programmes has a similar influence on the directions in which local partnerships in different countries focus their activities - on problems of unemployment, on the social dimensions of exclusion, or on a more integrated approach to local regeneration.

Alongside the role of government programmes supporting local partnerships, the relative effectiveness with which **different welfare systems** have coped with problems of poverty and social exclusion appears to be one important factor in the extent to which a local partnership approach has been adopted in different Member States. The pressures on the welfare state are both perceived and real. They concern both the 'scissors effect' of growing demands on state welfare and a fiscal or tax crisis, and criticisms of the effectiveness of the state in addressing complex social and economic questions, such as social exclusion. These pressures have been felt as both a need for new and complementary sources of funding for social and welfare policies, and a receptiveness to alternative forms of provision, by both the for-profit and the not-for-profit sectors. However, the degree of pressure on, and change to, the welfare state does not correlate in a simple fashion with the prominence of local partnership. A 'mixed market' of providers may develop through collaboration between providers on a primarily non-local basis, and at local level inter agency working, public-private collaboration, and involvement of users and consumers need not take a formal partnership shape.

Local partnerships have become an important dimension of the policy framework in countries with liberal welfare systems such as the UK which have aggressively promoted a mixed market of welfare provision. On the other hand, the partnership approach is less established in those states with either social democratic or corporatist welfare systems, although in both cases the more recent pressures upon them seem to be associated with a new interest in partnership working. In the same southern European countries, local partnership is increasingly seen as a way of extending what are relatively poorly developed welfare systems, in the current context of fiscal constraint.

Chapter 4

Local Partnership Across the European Union: Diversity and Common Themes

Introduction

The previous chapter has described the different contexts for local partnerships in each Member State, and the different extent to which local partnerships have been developed. This chapter, in contrast, will be primarily concerned with similarities and differences in experiences of local partnerships seeking to combat exclusion across the Member States of the European Union. It shows **how** local partnerships originate, **where** they are located, **who** is involved, **what** they do and on **which** *resources* they draw.

The chapter is based on the examples of local partnerships identified by the research, 86 in all, (including the 30 detailed case studies carried out in by the national research teams in ten of the member states), to survey the development and experience of local partnerships concerned with exclusion and poverty across the EU. The 86 local partnerships were selected to include a range of partnerships in each country conforming as closely as possible to the working definition of local partnerships described in Chapter 1, which tries to avoid the loose way in which the term 'partnership' is often used and find examples of partnerships which are more than inter-agency collaboration. As far as possible therefore the selection process identified partnerships with formal organisational structures, with partners from the public sector, employers and trade unions (the social partners), and the voluntary and community sectors, adopting a multidimensional approach to problems of unemployment, poverty and social exclusion. In addition, the selection was made to include local partnerships in different types of location, and associated with different EU, national and local government programmes. It is important to emphasise this basis for the research in relation to the following analysis.

Summary information about all the local partnerships identified in the research, including those where case studies were undertaken, is given in Appendix III.

The Origins of Local Partnerships

How do local partnerships develop? The research shows that the impetus for the formation of local partnerships can come from many sources:

- grassroots initiative, by local communities and their organisations;

- initiatives by employers or trade unionists acting at national or local level;

- initiative from local or regional government and public agencies;

- encouragement (including the possibility of funding) from national governments and ministries, or a requirement for a partnership to be established as a condition for funding;

- opportunities offered or conditions imposed by EU programmes.

Initiatives taken at **the local level** have often been the starting point of the process of establishing a partnership. This may have been initiative from **grassroots** community organisations, or from local public bodies, as the following examples illustrate.

Partnerships from the grassroots

Faced with the prospect of being resettled by the government of the GDR, the inhabitants of the small village of Wulkow (population 130) in Brandenburg near the Polish border had two options: to abandon their village or to fight for its future. The community mounted an initiative to revitalise their locality. In 1990, following reunification, they set up a partnership, the *Okospeicher*, which included almost every inhabitant: farmers, commuters, the mayor, traders, the school and the church.

The *IN LOCO* partnership in the Algarve, Portugal, resulted from the initiative of a group of teachers concerned about problems of social isolation and the decline of educational facilities, who gained financial support from a foreign charitable foundation.

Pavee Point, in Dublin, Ireland is an association founded on partnership principles by the Irish traveller community, and professionals working with them.

Frequently, it has been **local and regional government,** often acting closely with other public agencies and with the community and voluntary sectors, which has taken the lead in establishing partnerships.

Initiatives by local public authorities

The partnership in *Coventry and Warwickshire* in the UK was created on the initiative of the two main local authorities in the sub-region, and other local agencies, especially the Training and Enterprise Council. The partnership initiative was stimulated by the recognition by the local authorities that collaboration would increase their prospects of obtaining government funds for urban and rural regeneration.

The *Hanko* partnership in Finland started from the actions of officials in different departments of the local authority to promote more collective approaches to youth crime.

In other cases, the initiative has come from the *social partners*, sometimes nationally and sometimes at the local level, in the form of action by individual employers and trade unionists.

Initiatives by the social partners

In *Rennes* in France the CFDT trade union adopted a partnership approach in initiatives to combat social exclusion and unemployment. A number of projects have been developed to encourage labour market integration, with the co-operation of numerous actors and financial support from employers, financial institutions and the public sector.

The *Dortmund Development Centre* partnership began with initiatives by trade unions and trade unionists aimed at developing new socially useful products.

In Belgium, the *0.18-0.25% programme* is a joint initiative by employers and trade unions for a levy on the overall wage bill to fund projects to reintegrate groups experiencing exclusion.

The *Women's Foundation, Steyr,* Austria, resulted from initiative by women trade unionists in response to high levels of female unemployment resulting from industrial restructuring.

Sometimes it appears that the primary impetus for the formation of a local partnership has come not from the local area itself but from the opportunity offered by **national or regional government programmes.** National government programmes such as the Contrat de Ville programme in France and the City Challenge programme in the United Kingdom are leading examples of government programmes which have had an important role in stimulating and funding large scale local partnership projects. The Irish government has promoted a number of programmes based on a local partnership approach, including the Area Based Response to Long Term Unemployment, the Local Enterprise Programme, and the Programme for Integrated Development. In Belgium, Spain and Austria, regional governments have led the way in taking developing programmes which support local partnership approaches to combat economic and social exclusion.

The influence of national and regional governments

The *Dundalk Employment Partnership* in Ireland was stimulated by the Irish government's area based response to long-term unemployment programme.

In 1990 the Flemish government established the Flemish Fund for the Integration of the Underprivileged (VFIK) under which 15 municipalities, including *Beringen*, developed multidimensional local anti-poverty strategies.

In the Basque country (where the *Plan Vasco* partnership is located) and Catalonia, the regional governments have led the way in developing integrated global plans to combat poverty and exclusion, involving partnership between regional, provincial and local administrations, together with economic and social interests; and drawing on principles from the EU's Poverty 3 programme.

In southern European countries, such as Greece, Spain and Portugal, and also in Ireland, where the scale of EU funding has been significant, **European programmes** have been a leading influence in promoting models of local partnership. Important EU programmes have been the recently-completed Poverty 3 and LEDA social action programmes, LEADER I and II, and other recent Community Initiatives such as NOW and HORIZON (now part of the Employment Community Initiative).

The stimulus of European programmes

European programmes have played a particularly important role in Greece in introducing the concept and practice of local partnership. Examples include the Poverty 3-supported project in *Perama* and the New

Opportunities for Women partnership in *West Attica* project supported by the NOW programme.

The LEADER I programme appears, from the research studies in *South Kerry* in Ireland, the *Western Isles and Skye and Lochalsh* in northern Scotland, the *IN LOCO* partnership in southern Portugal and the *GALCOB* partnership in Brittany, to have been associated with the particularly successful development of a local partnership approach.

The origins of local partnerships also lie in a positive *combination* of these impetuses: collaboration between a local community, local public authorities and other national or local public agencies; stimulated by the prospect of funding from national or EU programmes.

Ireland is one of several countries where the initiative for many local partnerships has come from a combination of actors. The *Tallaght Partnership* stemmed from collaboration between grassroots initiative and a national government programme. The *South Kerry Development Partnership* originated in a combination of local initiative and the influence of the EU's LEADER programme. The *Paul Partnership, Limerick,* had its roots in the support given to local community initiative by the EU's Poverty 3 programme.

A general conclusion at this point is that the most fertile conditions for the emergence of strong local partnerships is where there is potential for positive collaboration between:

*   local communities and excluded groups

*   local public authorities and or other local interests, including employers and trade unions

*   government and EU programmes.

Geographical and socio-economic contexts

Local partnerships have been developed effectively in many locations where poverty and exclusion are geographically concentrated. These range from inner city and peripheral urban housing estates, to old industrial regions and rural regions and localities. While the clear majority of the partnerships described in the research are in urban areas, nearly a quarter are in rural areas. Some partnerships relate to quite small neighbourhoods and communities, others to more extensive urban and rural regions.

Not surprisingly, there is very often a close linkage between the formation of a local partnership and a local socio-economic crisis, causing or exacerbating unemployment, poverty and social exclusion in a particular area. The local partnerships in *Wulkow,* the small village in Germany whose continued existence was threatened by the collapse of employment and state planning policies; *Wedding* in Berlin and *Se and S Nicolau in Porto*, both deprived inner city districts, and *Onyar Est, Girona*, a deprived area in a prosperous town, are good examples of situations in which local communities, though threatened by serious social and economic problems, retained sufficient social cohesion and purpose for partnership relationships to develop.

But this does not always happen, and the reasons why 'local crisis' does not always spark a partnership response are important, but not always easy to identify. It may for example be that where poverty and exclusion are long-established and chronic - the consequence of generations of underdevelopment - it is particularly hard to mobilise collaborative responses. Similarly where unemployment and poverty is more spatially diffused and hidden, as in some rural areas, and local leadership is less forthcoming, a partnership response may not emerge.

The Poverty 3-funded partnership in *Granby-Toxteth* on Merseyside in the UK was established in an area where social divisions are deep and entrenched, both within local communities and in relations between local communities and public agencies. This posed serious problems in establishing an effective working partnership.

The *El Ribeiro* partnership in Galicia in Spain was located in an area of dispersed rural population where inter-communal distrust is common and public authorities are regarded with considerable distrust. Here again partnership proved very difficult to establish.

The partners

The interests represented in the local partnerships are extremely diverse. However it may be suggested that the local partnerships included in the research fall into four main groups:

1. Broad, multi-partner partnerships, including representation of public, private, voluntary and community interests. This is, for example, the

dominant model in local partnerships in the UK and Ireland and in many local partnerships supported by EU programmes. Of course there is considerable variety as to how and to what extent these main partner categories are represented.

2. Partnerships in which the main partners are the public, voluntary and community sectors. This category includes both partnerships between the public sector and substantial not-for-profit agencies, and others in which the core of partnership is between local voluntary and community organisations and public agencies.

3. Partnerships wholly or very largely among public sector authorities and agencies.

4. Partnerships in which the main partners are the social partners and state agencies. These local partnerships replicate national corporatist traditions at the local or regional level.

Table 4.1 shows the extent to which different partner interests are present in the local partnerships included in the research.

The **public sector** is represented in the great majority of the partnerships identified in the research, reflecting the primary responsibilities of the public sector for social policies.

Table 4.1 The main partners in local partnerships in the research

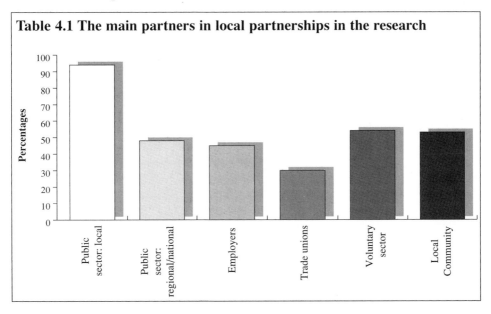

Local authorities are partners in many of the partnerships studied. In some countries, the participation of different tiers of government in **'vertical partnership',** from the **local to the regional and national,** is also a major feature. Alongside local authorities, **other local public or quasi-public agencies** (for example universities, or training organisations) are also frequently represented in partnerships.

Two partnerships in the UK illustrate a close relationship between local authorities and other local agencies, and the advantages to them from the formation of a local partnership. Coventry City Council and Warwickshire County Council are the leading players in the *Coventry and Warwickshire Partnership* in England, along with Coventry and Warwickshire Training And Enterprise Council, and second tier district authorities, in a broad local partnership which also includes employer, trade union and voluntary and community interests. In the *Western Isles and Skye and Lochalsh LEADER* partnership, the Local Enterprise Companies take the lead role, in close collaboration with the Western Isles Islands Council and Skye and Lochalsh District Council, alongside an NGO and a small farmers' association. In both partnerships, the local authorities are represented by both elected politicians and professional officers.

National government departments, ministries and agencies are partners in about two thirds of the partnerships studied. This can give local partnerships more effective access to national decision making and resources. For national agencies, local partnerships can offer effective mechanisms for implementing policies at the local level, and drawing in other actors and resources.

The City Contract of Lille is an example of a partnership which brings together partners primarily from the public and quasi-public sector, at regional, municipal and district levels, but also the local community and associations. The current partners include representatives of national/regional authorities:

• the State (the Regional Prefect)

• the Regional Council for Nord/Pas de Calais

• the Departmental Prefect and the sub-prefect in the city of municipal authorities:

• the Lille conurbation

• the Lille Urban Planning Agency

- the Communaute Urbaine de Lille

- the City of Lille and of local areas:

- districts within Lille, including elected politicians and community councils.

- local residents and associations.

There is **employer representation** in almost half of the local partnerships identified in the research. Employer involvement is increasingly promoted by EU programmes, and by some national government programmes, and may involve either individual employers or employer organisations. Representatives may be directors or owners of businesses, human resources managers or professional and/or technical staff with specific skills relevant to a partnership or part of its activity programme, such as financial or project planning skills.

The EU's LEADER programme, for example, was designed to promote entrepreneurship in rural areas. In the LEADER I local partnerships in *Brittany (GALCOB)*, the *Western Isles and Skye and Lochalsh* in Scotland, and to a lesser extent in *South Kerry,* employers and employer organisations were involved at a variety of levels: on management committees and sub-committees dealing with specific facets of the partnerships' activity, and in individual projects. The availability of LEADER funding to support projects proposed by the local business communities had much to do with the involvement of employers.

In local partnerships in Ireland, which have been supported by national policy programmes, employer representation has taken place on the basis of a numerical formula agreed at national level between government and the social partners. In the United Kingdom, successive policy programmes, principally City Challenge and the Single Regeneration Budget Challenge Fund, have promoted public-private sector partnership.

North Tyneside City Challenge Partnership is a broad, multi-partner partnership in which the Business Forum is one of five constituencies with equal representation on the partnership's Board. The Housing Forum includes construction companies, and the Economic Assembly includes economic development agencies in which private sector interests are strongly represented.

Often however the involvement of employers is dependent on whether businesses consider that the objectives and approaches of specific local initiatives are relevant to them, and this can mean that employer representation is either absent or limited.

> The *BRUTEC* partnership in Brussels includes the social partners, public authorities and local associations. It provides training and other support to enable individuals from excluded groups to gain access to new and high-tech employment. The partnership depends on the willingness of employers to offer jobs to trainees, and there have been positive results for businesses which have participated. However the limited nature of employer support remains one of the major issues facing the partnership.

Trade union involvement is a feature of only about one third of the partnerships in the research. However trade unions are actively involved in a number of local partnerships, where the emphasis is on unemployment and the regeneration of the local economy, for example in the partnership which was supported by the recent LEDA programme in *St Etienne.* or the *Dundalk Partnership* and other local partnership companies in Ireland, where trade union representation derives from a formula established by national agreement.

Trade union involvement may be in the form of the involvement of individual trade unionists, as in the partnerships in *Wedding* in Germany, and the *Alma Mater Centre* in Turin, or more formal organisational participation, as in the partnership initiatives in *Rennes* in France, or the *Fonds pour l'Emploi* in Belgium, where the core of local partnership is between the social partners, with the support of public authorities.

Trade unions have also played an active role in local partnerships in Germany and Austria concerned with issues of employment and training.

> The *Association for the Promotion of New Production, Kiel*, was set up in 1986 on the initiative of a group connected with the metal industry trade union IG Metall. The core members of the partnership are drawn from works councils and trade unions, but there is close collaboration with partners from the public and voluntary sectors. The *Dortmund Development Centre* was also formed as a trade union response to industrial restructuring and interest in the development of new socially useful products, although over time the trade union contribution to the partnership has diminished.

In Austria, the *Labour Foundation Programme in Carinthia*, and the *Women's Foundation in Steyr* both centre on collaboration between the social partners at regional level. The latter is a particularly notable example of initiative by women trade unionists to promote new employment opportunities for women which has gained wide support from the public authorities.

Voluntary sector organisations are represented in over half of the partnerships studied. Several examples illustrate the varied contribution of the voluntary sector to local partnerships.

The *ARCIL* partnership in Lousa, Portugal is concerned with the needs of disabled children. ARCIL is founded on local voluntary associations, and the partnership links these with public sector agencies, and with other sources of funding, including EU programmes, for the delivery of integrated care for the local population.

The *Alma Mater* project in Turin for immigrant women, was awarded an EU prize in 1994 as a model action to promote the integration of non-EU immigrants. On the basis of voluntary action, in conjunction with the local public authorities, the project provides a centre for immigrant women with multidimensional support functions.

Both these partnerships typify the role played by local voluntary organisations, especially in southern Europe, where welfare has traditionally depended heavily on the non-governmental sector.

Several partnership programmes in Belgium, such as the *Summer Programme for Young People*, while initiated by regional public authorities, have led to a greater role for voluntary organisations in partnership with both the public sector and employers.

In Finland, Denmark and Sweden, voluntary organisations concerned with specific social groups such as the mentally ill, the disabled and alcohol and drug abusers have played leading roles in local partnership projects. The Freezehouse in Stockholm, a centre for youth activities and training , was the result of initiatives by individuals working with young people in local sports and leisure associations.

The involvement of **local community organisations and interests** as partners is a feature of about half the local partnerships in the research.

In the *Okospeicher* partnership in Wulkow, a high proportion of the local community are directly involved as individual members of the partnership association.

In several partnerships supported by the *Poverty 3* programme, such as those in *Porto* and *Brownlow*, local community interests occupied a powerful position in the partnership.

In the *North Tyneside City Challenge Partnership*, representatives elected from local community forums constitute one of five interests with equal representation in numerical terms on the partnership's board.

In the partnership in *Beringen* in Belgium, local community associations were represented in the partnership management board, and the partnership also used neighbourhood meetings to involve local people.

In local partnership companies in Ireland, a nationally-derived formula gives the local community parity of representation with other interests.

However the direct representation of community interests as partners is not a feature of all local partnerships. In some, local interests are indirectly represented by elected local politicians, or even more indirectly by officials from local public authorities. Local communities and excluded groups may only be consulted or represented in specific projects, but not in the main partnership structure.

Most local partnerships in the research do not have formal *equal opportunities* policies which would establish and implement principles concerning the extent to which women, ethnic minorities and other disadvantaged groups are involved in them (as partner representatives or employees), and in what positions of power and influence.

A common situation in practice in many partnerships is for women to occupy many positions within the partnership, but for management roles to be dominated by men, as for example in the Brownlow Community Trust.

In the *Brownlow Community Trust* in Northern Ireland, the project team was led by a woman and women made up a majority of the staff. On the project's Board, there were roughly equal numbers of male and female political and community representatives. However nine out of ten representatives of public sector agencies were men.

In Ireland however, a quota system requiring local partnerships to include at least 40% of each gender among partner representatives has recently been introduced and support materials developed to encourage awareness of the issue (Area Development Management 1996).

The *ARCIL* partnership in Lousa, Portugal, is concerned with provision for people with disabilities. While those with disabilities are not represented on the Management Board, which comprises representatives of specialists, parents and other community interests, ARCIL has created 61 'sheltered employment' posts in the organisation and developed many projects providing employment for people with disabilities.

The **legal frameworks** and **organisational structures** of local partnerships condition the ways in which different interests are represented, and have a major impact on the effectiveness of partnerships in developing and implementing effective strategies and action plans. The structure with which a partnership works may not be a question of local choice, but may be determined by the provisions of national or EU funding programmes. In other cases there has been considerable local initiative in seeking to devise suitable frameworks and structures.

Not surprisingly, in some of the small partnerships, organisational structures are simple. But larger partnerships with multiple partners, complex action programmes and significant budgets have had to develop sophisticated structures for representation and management. Despite this diversity, many of the partnerships identified by the research exhibit a similar structure:

- A management or partnership board, which has both representational and managerial/strategic functions.

- Subcommittees or similar groups which oversee or undertake specific facets of the partnership's work.

- A project team, which again is frequently disaggregated into several sub-teams according to different areas of activity undertaken by the partnership.

A formal, legal framework for local partnerships, independent of that of partner organisations, is important for partnerships to manage their own funding, and to employ staff. Many partnerships thus take the form of a not-for-profit association or limited liability company.

The formal partnership structures through which partnerships operate coexist with wider and more diffuse patterns of collaboration and networking between local organisations and in local communities. Thus, as the Portuguese research suggests, many partnerships involve a dynamic oscillation between *'partenariado'* (formal partnership) and *'parceria'* (informal partnership), in which the formal partnership provides an umbrella for informal partnerships, but is in its turn sustained by the informal networks of interaction.

The focus of partnership activity

Local partnerships vary greatly in the scope and focus of their strategies, action plans and activities. Many are part of European or national programmes with defined objectives and concerns; but others are the product of more local, 'bottom up' initiative. In the former, the emphasis is often on the delivery of largely determined programmes, while the latter are frequently more open-ended and developmental, while more limited in their resources.

There has been a growing policy consensus that programmes to combat exclusion need to be multidimensional in their scope, including a concern with:

• economic development and job creation

• training and education

• physical, housing and environmental renewal

• public service provision

• income and welfare support

• community safety and crime prevention

• health

• community development

A multidimensional approach to building social cohesion and combating poverty, and unemployment was central to the local partnerships in the Poverty 3 programme. National programmes such as the Neighbourhood Social Development programme (DSQ - Development Sociale des Quartiers) in France, the National Anti-Poverty Programme in Portugal, the City Challenge and Single Regeneration Budget programmes in the UK, and Irish government programmes such as the Programme for Integrated Development, have shared many of the partnership, participation and multidimensionality themes of Poverty 3.

The *Onyar Est Partnership* in Girona, Spain, achieved particular success in mobilising a large number of the city's players and sectors who had previously had little involvement in combating poverty and social exclusion. In particular, the partnership achieved a notable advance in moving from a primarily social agenda to action against unemployment, with excellent results in labour market integration of the unemployed as a result of the development of an effective dialogue with employers.

The *Okospeicher* partnership in Wulkow represents a remarkable example of an integrated and multidimensional approach at the very local level of a small village.

However even within a broad multidimensional approach there can be significant differences of breadth, depth and focus: from physical renewal of poor neighbourhoods, to community and social development, and economic development and employment.

The current research shows though (see Table 4.2) that the 'multidimensional' approach to social exclusion is paralleled by other local partnerships in which activity is focused on more specific issues. These latter may be divided into two broad categories:

- those focusing on unemployment, employment and economic development;

- those concerned with aspects of social services provision, including housing, and with community development.

Secondly, some partnerships adopt an area or community-based approach, while others target their activities at particular social groups, such as women, young people, and other social groups, including ethnic groups, people with disabilities.

Local partnerships concerned with **employment, training and economic development** may be involved in a range of activities, including:

- the attraction of new businesses to deprived areas;

- support for existing local employers, and the promotion of entrepreneurship and job creation in the local economy;

- education, training and labour market support programmes to improve the job prospects of local communities and excluded groups;

- renewal or enhancement of physical infrastructure to support economic development.

Table 4.2 The focus of partnership activity

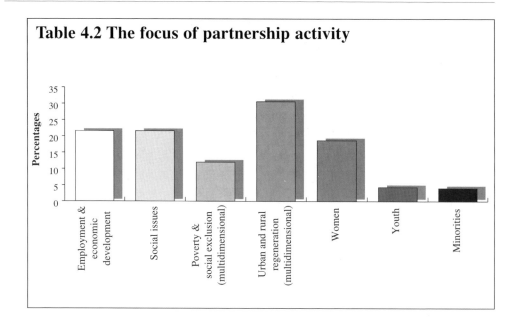

The *North Tyneside City Challenge Partnership* is one of the best resourced local partnerships analysed in the research, with a remit and a level of funding which has allowed it (alongside other local projects) to undertake a wide range of infrastructural, promotional and labour market activities to promote employment and economic development.

BRUTEC (Brussels Association for training in new technologies and employment promotion) is a partnership between a number of training initiatives targeted at excluded groups, representatives of the social partners, and of public training bodies. The partnership links four initiatives in poor areas of Brussels to identify new job opportunities associated with new technologies and by working with companies in the relevant sectors make them accessible to the young unemployed with poor qualifications.

Partnerships in rural areas funded by the LEADER programme have given particular emphasis to promoting local entrepreneurship in areas where this has traditionally proved difficult and where local cultures of dependence on state welfare have been regarded as entrenched.

Local partnership arrangements are increasingly important in **social service provision** as a 'mixed market' of providers becomes more common. The research includes numerous examples of local partnerships concerned with aspects of social service provision from housing to healthcare and in relation to specific social problems such as alcohol and drug abuse. Several examples illustrate a local partnership approach in this area.

The *Ballymun Task Force*, on a housing estate to the north of Dublin, represents a model approach to public housing policy in Ireland. Ballymun is an area of high-rise housing, now in poor condition and tenanted by high proportions of lone parents, single and formerly homeless people. The Task Force emerged as a community response to this housing crisis by a campaigning group of residents. This has led to the establishment of a partnership comprised of representatives from the public health and housing authorities, the Community Coalition and tenants' associations.

The *Castlemilk Partnership*, in Glasgow, is one of the local partnerships supported by the UK government's New Life for Urban Scotland programme. Castlemilk, like Ballymun, is a large, run down, peripheral housing estate. The partnership combines the Scottish Office of the government, local authorities, housing, health and economic development agencies, and a private sector business group.

The *Vuosaari* partnership in an eastern suburb of Helsinki illustrates the contribution which partnership can make in the context of new housing development, rather than the renewal of rundown estates. The Vuosaari project was set up as the area was being developed, with the aim of preventing the emergence of problems typical of large new housing developments. It has involved partnership working between national housing and social welfare bodies and local authority departments, and a residents committee

Other social dimensions of exclusion tackled by local partnerships include both 'mainstream' social provision, and specific social problems such as alcoholism.

The Social Services and Health Care Districts initiative in the Tyrol, Austria, has created partnership working between local authorities, general practitioners, the Red Cross and individuals active in the local community on social matters. There is increasing demand for mobile care and medical services in this rural area, especially from old people, and the initiative provides a formal organisational structure, a focal point of contact and a multi-purpose centre through which tight resources can be co-ordinated and developed, including self-help and the assistance of non-professionals.

The *Sirkkulanpuisto Action Group* in Kuopio, Finland, is an association supporting those suffering from alcohol and drug abuse, especially the homeless. The Group was set up, with funding from the Ministry of the

Environment and the national Slot Machine Association, because of the limitations of official responses to these problems, and to assist these excluded groups in solving their own problems. It has developed a working partnership between the local authorities at parish, municipal and regional level, the local university, local vocational schools of social work and health, the association for the unemployed, and some private employers.

Partnerships have responded to the specific needs of *women* in two main ways. Some partnerships have been focused exclusively on the needs of women, or particular groups of women, while in others there has been a focus on women as a specific group within broader partnership strategies.

In the *Brownlow Community Trust* in Northern Ireland, the partnership's strategy and activity plan focused on the needs of three groups: women, children and the unemployed. The partnership addressed women's needs in a number of ways: through the specific projects undertaken; through the gender perspective in the strategy as a whole; through the leading role given to women in partnership structures and processes; and through the impact of the partnership's approach on partner agencies. The action plan included several major initiatives for women, such as a Women's Forum and a health project.

A further group of partnerships have focused on women's needs in more defined contexts. The New Opportunities for Women partnership in *West Attica*, Greece, set up a vocational training and employment centre for women. The partnership which supported the *Alma Mater* centre in Turin has been initiated and led by immigrant women, and has succeeded in gaining the support of a range of partners, including trade unions and public sector agencies for a developing strategy offering a range of support to women immigrants.

The *Women's Foundation* in Steyr, Austria, is a response to the problems of female unemployment, particularly for older women and those with lower skill levels, caused by processes of industrial restructuring. As existing training was inadequate, an initiative was taken by women trade unionists and politicians to offer more comprehensive help. This 'women's coalition' received strong support at regional and national levels, and set up a Foundation, funded largely by public sector authorities, with wide objectives of promoting equal opportunity and facilitating the return of unemployed women to the labour market. The Foundation is largely run by women, and includes partners from the trade unions and local and provincial government.

As with the gender dimensions of exclusion, some partnerships have prioritised actions for **children and young people** within broader multidimensional partnership strategies, while other partnerships have developed, and been more specifically focused around, youth issues.

The *Iisalmi Youth Support Group*, the *Young People's Workshop* in Joutseno and *the Hanko Shadow Group*, all in Finland, show how partnership working can enhance responses to issues of youth unemployment and crime. The Iisalmi project provides interesting and meaningful work for unemployed young people in danger of becoming excluded. The Joutseno project aims to break the cycle of unemployment and temporary employment by finding education, training and apprenticeships for school leavers. The Hanko project supports children and young families in a town where poor employment prospects are leading to increasing levels of crime and delinquency.

Several partnership projects are concerned with minorities and other excluded groups, such as individuals suffering from alcohol or drug abuse, for example the *Gothenburg City Mission Foundation*. The *ARCIL* partnership in Portugal, and the *Norrkoping Business Network* in Sweden are examples of partnership to improve the employment opportunities of those with disabilities or psycho-social problems. While in the former local community organisations have had a formative role, the latter shows the leading role which employers (both private and public) and trade unions can play in preventing the exclusion of certain groups.

Pavee Point is a Dublin-based partnership which works with travellers. Travellers often depend on social welfare, and their high risk of poverty is compounded by their primitive housing and living conditions, often resulting in low life expectancy rates. Pavee Point is a partnership organisation consisting of travellers and settled people working together in partnership to promote the well being of travellers. Initially funded as a training agency, it has diversified its activities with support from the former Poverty 3 programme, EU Community Initiatives, and the Irish government. Pavee Point has succeeded in developing partnership relationships which both enable travellers to exercise management and control while creating a bridge between them and the settled community, the public sector and other organisations.

Financial resources

The main direct funding for the 86 local partnerships identified came from regional and local authorities, national governments and EU programmes.

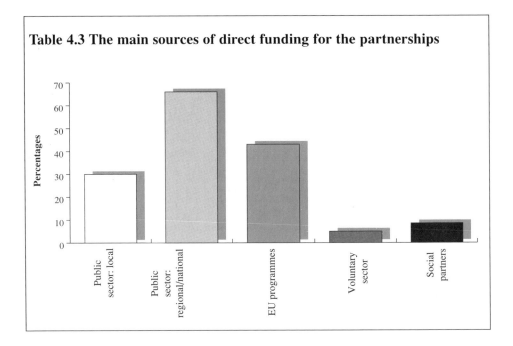

Table 4.3 The main sources of direct funding for the partnerships

A few of these programmes, such as the UK City Challenge and Single Regeneration Budget or the French Contrat de Ville, enable a minority of local partnerships to access significant financial resources, amounting to several tens of million ECUs over a period of about five years. Funding from EU Community Initiatives and social action programmes such as LEADER and Poverty 3, however, is normally seen in the context of pilot or experimental funding, and is therefore at a significantly lesser level, although it may still be very significant at the local level.

In general though, funding for local partnerships from either EU or national governments is relatively small in relation to mainstream social or economic policy expenditure by governments, or the EU's Structural Funds. Major programme funding from employers, trade unions or the voluntary sector is much less usual, although important examples of funding by the social partners include the 0.15% programme in Belgium and the Carinthian Labour

Foundation in Austria. For some smaller partnerships funding from charitable foundations is important. However, in many cases, state funding (from governments, the EU or regional or local authorities) has to be paralleled by matching funding from other partners, including private firms, public sector bodies and voluntary organisations.

The overall scale of this is difficult to estimate, but in some cases, such as some LEADER partnerships, the 'matching' funding significantly exceeds that obtained from the programme.

The *Western Isles and Skye and Lochalsh LEADER* I programme significantly exceeded its own targets for levering in matching funding. £1.4m was allocated from the LEADER programme, with a forecast that this would produce overall expenditure of £3.3m together with additional public and private funding. In the event this was easily exceeded, with overall funding of £4.9m.

Other sources of funding, including income from activities undertaken or supported by the partnership, are less significant in the overall picture but important nonetheless for individual partnerships. Another financial contribution is often the unpaid work which many partner representatives and others contribute, which if it had to be undertaken by paid staff would amount to a significant budget item.

Local partnerships may depend on programme funding, and/or funding for specific projects. This can influence whether partnerships have adequate funding to support the operation of the partnership itself. In the UK, for example, local actors can incur very significant and unfunded costs in establishing a partnership framework as a precondition for applying for local regeneration funding, and the competitive nature of resource allocation means that there is no guarantee that these 'pump priming' resources will bear fruit. A further consideration is that the financial resources available to local partnership projects can involve substantial new funding or merely the reallocation of existing resources (or even, in some cases, a reduction of previous resourcing). Many of the sources of funding for local partnerships are short-term, reflecting factors such as their status as pilot or experimental initiatives from the point of view of funding bodies or programmes. However as a result many more established partnerships have had to develop strategies to diversify and replace initial funding sources, as the example of the Paul Partnership in Ireland illustrates:

Programme funding received by the Paul Partnership 1990-1995

Programme	Time period	Amount (£)
EU Poverty 3	1990-1994	1,616,975
Area Based Partnership funding (ABR)	1991-1994	286,000
Money Advice Programme	1992-1995	125,000
EU Horizon	1992-1994	160,300
Enterprise Trust	1992-1994	36,600
EU Global Grant	1992-1994	440,000
Community Development Programme	1994-1995	50,000
EU Local Development Programme	1995	395,547
Local Employment Service funding	1995	263,000

Conclusion

This chapter has identified key features of the local partnership approach to problems of poverty and exclusion across the Member States of the EU:

- The research shows that local partnerships can be a flexible tool in combating economic and social exclusion, adaptable to different contexts. Local partnerships have been developed in many different types of location where such problems are geographically concentrated, including inner city and peripheral urban locations and rural areas. Some partnerships relate to quite small neighbourhoods, others to wide regional and sub-regional areas.

- The impetus for the formation of local partnerships comes often from local initiative, but also from the requirements of national and regional government and EU programmes, and the funding they offer. Greater strength can come from a combination of 'bottom up' and 'top down' initiative, in which either locally-rooted initiatives seek funding from outside the 'local' area, or EU and national programmes stimulate local initiative.

- The involvement of the public sector, especially local authorities and agencies, is almost universal in partnerships. The involvement of other partners is strongly related to the content of the partnership's activity.

Community interests and excluded groups are frequently not directly represented in partnership structures.

• The main funding for local partnerships also comes from the public sector, either local, national or European. Lead funding from other partners is much less usual. Sustaining a partnership often means drawing together funding from several sources over a period of time.

• In many of the local partnerships researched, the objectives and activities of the partnership are broadly based, involving a multidimensional approach to poverty and social exclusion, local regeneration, social integration, or rural development. In a significant number however the remit is more specific, focusing on either economic or social dimensions of exclusion or the needs of specific social groups.

Chapter 5   Building Local Partnerships

Introduction

This chapter discusses the processes and working methods of building local partnerships. It is based primarily on the experience of the 30 case studies of local partnerships in the 10 member states where research studies were undertaken. These are shown in Table 5.1 and the map below. The case studies made use of existing documentation - such as evaluation or end of project reports prepared by or for the partnerships themselves - but the research teams also undertook programmes of interviews with those most involved in the local partnerships, especially representatives of partner organisations and members of partnership teams. The research is therefore able to reflect the views of policymakers and practitioners themselves on the experience of partnership working at the local level.

The case studies were undertaken to a standard, agreed framework. They concentrated on a number of broad areas of interest:

- The representation of interests in partnerships, and the relative influence of different partners;

- The process of negotiation and alliance building in developing a common strategy and action plan, and how and to what extent conflicts were resolved;

- The working methods developed by local partnerships, the skills which they required, and the resources to which they had access.

This chapter considers each of these issues in turn. In addition, the case studies were concerned with the impacts of local partnerships, which are discussed in the following chapter.

TABLE 5.1 The case studies of local partnerships

Austria	Women's Foundation, Steyr Social Services and Healthcare District 'Regions 12 and 13', Tyrol Carinthian Labour Foundation Programme
Belgium	Plan for Social Innovation, Beringen BRUTEC Partnership, Brussels Action for Social Co-ordination, La Louviere
Finland	Iisalmi Youth Support Group Hanko Varjopuoli Shadow Side Work Group Healthy Vuosaari
France	GALCOB Centre-Ouest Bretagne LEADER Contrat de Ville de Lille Mantes la Jolie Poverty 3
Germany	Ökospeicher, Wulkow Communales Forum, Wedding, Berlin EWZ Dortmund
Greece	West Attica Development Association Perama (Poverty 3) Social Exclusion of Muslim minorities
Ireland	Tallaght Partnership South Kerry Development Partnership Paul Partnership, Limerick
Portugal	Projecto Zona Historico Se e S Nicolau, Porto Associacao IN LOCO, Algarve ARCIL (Associacao para a Recuperao de Cidadaos Inadaptados da Lousa)
Spain	Onyar Est, Girona El Ribeiro, Galicia Plan Vasco, Alava (Basque Country Global Plan to Combat Poverty)
United Kingdom	Western Isles and Skye and Lochalsh LEADER North Tyneside City Challenge Partnership Coventry and Warwickshire Partnerships

Location of Case Studies of Local Partnerships

Representation

The negotiation of an alliance of organisations, actors and interests with the aim of implementing a common strategy and action plan is the essential basis for partnership working. This implies two requirements: first, the effective representation of key interests in partnership structures, and, second, the negotiation of an effective alliance between the key actors. The chapter looks at each of these in succession, starting with extent to which different interests have been successfully represented in the case study partnerships.

Representational structures

In a few of the partnerships researched, especially those with a strong grassroots element, the main forum in which different actors and interests were represented took the form of an **association with a wide membership.** In the Okospeicher partnership in Germany, to take a prominent example, this association had 150 members, including both local and external interests, of whom 50 were (mostly small or very small) businesses, 70 were individuals, 16 were institutes of different sorts and 14 were from the university sector. This kind of open membership forum has advantages of access for many interests, but often leads to much of the practical leadership being in the hands of one or a few prominent individuals.

In the majority of the partnerships the main (although not the only) forum in which interests are represented is a **partnership board or management committee,** in which membership is not open but is designed to secure particular patterns of interest representation. Several examples can illustrate the different balances of representation which are characteristic of many of the partnerships. The board of directors of the Tallaght Partnership in Ireland is based on a 'quadripartite' pattern of representation, in which the four key interests are defined as those of the public sector, employers, trade unions, and the voluntary and community sector, which is applied in many Irish local partnerships, in a formula laid down in the PESP (Partnership for Economic and Social Planning) national agreement. In the Tallaght Partnership, this meant that the Board comprised six public sector partners, three each nominated by the national organisations representing the social partners plus two 'local social partners', six from the community sector and two from the voluntary sector. The partnership in Se and S Nicolau, in Porto, illustrates another concept of representation of interests, in this case also defining four key interests: state services (six representatives), local authorities (three), private social welfare institutions (six) and local community associations (two). The Board of the

North Tyneside City Challenge partnership is based on the identification of five interests or 'forums': the local authority, a business forum, a housing forum, an economic forum and a community forum. Each of the five forums supplies four members of the board, but they are chosen in different ways. Business partners are nominated by prominent employers but most of the community partners are elected from local housing estates.

All of the above examples are illustrative of forms of partner and interest representation characteristic of partnerships with broad, multidimensional programmes, requiring the representation of a wide variety of interests. In other partnerships with more limited areas of activity, the representation of interests tends accordingly to be narrower. The focus of the BRUTEC partnership in Brussels on training and employment is reflected in a Board structure made up of three categories: training organisations (50% of the membership), employers and trade unions (the social partners) (25%) and public bodies, mostly training-related (25%). The Women's Foundation in Steyr has the key partner interests from the trade unions and the local authority represented on its Executive Board, all of whose members are women. In such cases a 'narrower' representation of relevant interests can allow the representation of those interests in considerable numbers and depth.

In some partnerships, the representation of interests has been limited in order to maintain the perceived advantages of a small and 'tight' partnership. In the LEADER partnership in the Western Isles and Skye and Lochalsh, Scotland, membership was confined to local authorities and local enterprise companies and leading NGOs. Other NGOs were excluded from the formal representational structure in order not to threaten what was seen as a successful partnership framework. On the other hand, other partnerships have developed complex structures partly in order to offer representation to many interests. In some cases, an **Annual General Meeting or similar assembly** is used to offer some involvement to a wide membership, while 'core' partners sit on a management committee. In the Steyr Women's Foundation, the representation of local partners on the Executive Board is paralleled by an **Advisory Council** on which external stakeholders are represented. In other cases subcommittees of the main management committee are developed, partly for operational reasons as is discussed below, but partly to offer more opportunities for representation within the partnership. Some partnerships, such as the Paul Partnership, Ireland, which have gained funding from a number of programmes and sources over a period of time have had to restructure their representational bodies to adjust to the different demands made by funding programmes.

The research shows therefore that although a management board or committee is the most general forum used by partnerships to ensure a satisfactory balance of interest representation, local partnerships have adapted this mechanism in a wide variety of ways in order to meet their needs.

Key actors

Public Authorities

In many of the casestudy partnerships, **public sector organisations** are the most strongly represented interests, and are often the most powerful partners. This reflects both the predominantly public sources of funding for local partnerships, and the fact that problems of unemployment, poverty and social exclusion still remain primarily the responsibility of public authorities. This means that, in different contexts, partnerships may need to offer representation to a number of different public sector organisations, and/or to different interests within a particular organisation, such as a local authority, in order to promote inter-agency or cross-departmental working on joint problems.

Examples from the research illustrate the way in which partnerships have provided a framework for a wide range of public sector organisations to work in partnership. In the City Contract of Lille partnership, the availability of substantial resources for urban regeneration provided a context in which a successful partnership has been built involving representation from central, regional, urban and local state bodies, including both political representatives and officials. In Vuosaari and Hanko in Finland senior professionals from different local authority departments and other local public agencies are represented in the partnerships. Both regional and local authorities are important partners in the Social Services and Healthcare Districts in the Tyrol which have delivered a more integrated and customer-focused approach to service delivery. In North Tyneside, the local authority has played a leading role in the City Challenge partnership, in contrast to previous local regeneration initiatives in the locality which had been business-led. This required significant cultural and organisational change within the authority to adjust to a partnership approach, particularly with the private sector. **Local politicians** are key actors in the North Tyneside partnership, and also in the Onyar Est partnership in Girona, where active leadership by a 'new breed' of local elected politicians was one of the important factors in establishing a strong partnership in which key interests were represented effectively. In Ireland however local elected politicians are not participants in most local partnerships, although the problems this poses for local democratic accountability are now being recognised and addressed.

As well as local authorities, **other local state and quasi-state agencies** can play powerful roles on local partnership boards and management committees, particularly when their own role demands collaboration between the public and private sectors, as in the case of agencies concerned with employment and training. In the LEADER partnership in the Western Isles and Skye and Lochalsh, Scotland, the dominant partners were the local authorities and Local Enterprise Councils. The LECs - represented in the partnership by their Chief Executives and by members of their boards from the business community - took the leading role because the focus of LEADER on the promotion of enterprise was close to their own objectives. Initial reservations by local elected representatives about this because of the unelected status of the LECs were diminished by the process of collaboration within the partnership and growing perceptions of its value.

National/federal/regional government departments and agencies tend not to be directly represented in local partnerships, but in some countries, including Ireland, Austria, Portugal and Spain, such agencies can be powerful partners. The benefits of this involvement can be to bring the policies and resources of such agencies more closely into line with local needs and wishes. But the research shows that partnerships can experience considerable difficulties in drawing national agencies into partnership working in a positive way. The experience of partnerships such as those in South Kerry, Tallaght, and Porto illustrates a tendency for national state agencies to pursue their own interests in local partnerships, regarding partnership resources as a means of building their own 'empires', and demonstrating only limited adaptation to the culture of partnership. In Greece, the research study showed that, in a situation where government has been strongly centralised, this has created formidable obstacles to the effective participation of local authorities in partnerships. In Spain, the sharing of responsibilities between public authorities at different levels does not necessarily produce effective partnership between them, partly, the Spanish research suggests, because of the legacy of authoritarian rule.

Social Partners

The social partners are the dominant interests in only a small number of the local partnerships researched. In the Women's Foundation, Steyr, and the Labour Foundation partnership in Carinthia, the **trade unions** are the driving force of partnership, supported by the public authorities and employers. In the partnership in Dortmund, on the other hand, while trade unionists were instrumental in the early stages of the initiative, their role has declined as the focus of partnership activity and funding has shifted from a focus on new forms of socially useful production to more general training activity, illustrating the way in which the leadership and power in local partnerships is often closely associated with the sources of money.

In other cases, **businesses** play a very important role. The resources available to the North Tyneside City Challenge partnership have ensured the active participation of major private sector firms on the management board and in implementing the partnership strategy to regenerate the local area, which offers substantial commercial benefits, both direct and indirect, to businesses. In other partnerships there is active participation by smaller businesses. Small employers are important partners in some partnerships (such as the Okospeicher in Wulkow). Smaller firms may be represented through local business organisations such as **chambers of commerce and industry**, as in the partnership in Coventry and Warwickshire and some of the LEADER partnerships. It is also quite common for businesses to be involved in local partnerships through individual projects and activities, although they may not be represented in the primary partnership structures.

Undoubtedly, a major stimulus to social partner representation has been the influence of those national and EU funding programmes which make business representation a condition of access to funding. However the evidence from national reports such as those for the UK and Ireland, shows that in some cases this can lead to business/employer representation which is superficial or symbolic, and this can raise expectations which the partnership cannot then meet as to the contributions which businesses are likely to make.

Other partners have on occasion made major efforts to encourage the representation of social partner interests because of their importance in tackling unemployment and promoting local economic development. As the partnership in Onyar Est, Girona, began to integrate the economic and social dimensions of exclusion, initially-reluctant employers and trade unions were drawn in to contribute to employment and labour market policies. The BRUTEC partnership in Brussels has similarly devoted considerable energy to the involvement of businesses and trade unions because they are central to BRUTEC's objective of enabling individuals from excluded groups to access employment in high-tech jobs.

Other partnerships demonstrate some of the difficulties experienced by partnerships in securing the representation of social partner interests. All those local partnerships analysed in the Greek research experienced great difficulty in involving employers in partnerships concerned with poverty and social exclusion, as did those also within the Poverty 3 programme in Beringen and Porto. Some Irish partnerships, such as the Tallaght Partnership, reflect the problem that in many areas of poverty and social exclusion there are few substantial employers with the willingness or capacity to play a sustained role in local partnerships, despite the encouragement given by employer organisations nationally. Many local partnerships have also experienced difficulty in attracting active trade union participation at the local level, although the research points to some notable exceptions to this, including the active participation by local trade unionists in the partnerships in Wulkow and Wedding in Germany. The important point from these examples is that the involvement of trade unions sprang from the local activity and commitment of individuals, not from national trade union organisations.

In relation to the representation of the social partners, the research suggests, therefore, that effective representation of employers in local partnerships currently depends heavily on the degree to which the activities of partnerships are aligned to their own direct interests, in commercial opportunities or training for example. Partnerships may also have to make active efforts to search out employer partners if they want them. On the trade union side the notable examples of trade union involvement come out of either a context of collaboration at national level between the social partners and government, or from the grassroots involvement of local trade unionists.

Voluntary and Community Sectors

The research shows that **voluntary sector organisations** are strongly represented in local partnerships in two main contexts. The first - but the less common in the research - is where large voluntary organisations contribute to broadly based local partnerships. One example is the involvement of the Caritas charity in the Girona partnership, Onyar Est, where the Spanish research suggests that, although Caritas maintained a critical posture to the partnership, it adopted a pragmatic position, contributing to the partnership's action programme and according priority to its objectives. In the partnership in North Tyneside, voluntary organisations, including the national children's charity Barnardos, were represented in the partnership through a local voluntary resource centre, although they did not feel that this accorded them as central a role as they would have liked. Of considerably greater significance however appear to be those situations where locally rooted, often small, voluntary organisations have strong links to local populations and communities, and strong records of meeting the needs of disadvantaged groups and communities. In the ARCIL and IN LOCO partnerships in Portugal, locally based voluntary organisations and associations with close informal links to local communities were at the heart of the partnership framework. ARCIL - the Association for the Rehabilitation of People with Special Needs in Lousa (in central Portugal) developed from the initiative of a local group working with the disabled into an active partnership between the voluntary and public sectors, bringing together professional workers, the families of those with disabilities and wider local community involvement, and securing financial support from a range of EU and national programmes to support and undertake a complex programme of projects and activities for this disadvantaged group, while maintaining the local, grassroots orientation of the partnership.

In similar contexts, **community organisations and groups** have played a leading role. Three examples from the research are the partnerships in Wulkow and Wedding in Germany and ARCIL in Portugal, where grassroots community organisations and individuals are members of the partnership associations in large numbers, alongside other partners, both from the locality and outside the local area. These local partnerships have open, egalitarian and 'democratic' structures and working processes of 'horizontal partnership' at the local level, and have also developed effective 'vertical partnership' with national and European actors, both by participation in national and European programmes, and by development of national and transnational networks on their own initiative. Thus the Wulkow partnership has developed active links with Eastern European countries, and the IN LOCO partnership has a leading role in Portuguese local development networks. In instances such as these, partnership offers excluded groups and communities an institutional framework around which local solidarity can be organised, and external support and resources can be acquired in the struggle for local development and against poverty and exclusion.

In most partnerships in the research however community interests do not occupy positions of parity with other partners on partnership management committees or boards. In some cases, while community organisations and representatives do occupy positions in the partnership's structure and working processes, the research suggests that the core of the partnership was built between other partners, in a 'formal partnership' which tends to exclude or negate active community participation. The case studies of the partnerships in Se and S Nicolau in Porto, in Beringen, and in North Tyneside show how the formal structures of some partnerships, their operation according to the procedures familiar to formal organisations but less so to community organisations and disadvantaged groups, and the determination of their programmes (often a-priori) by the requirements and rhythms of European or national programmes, can work against the effective representation of community interests.

In local partnerships, such as BRUTEC and the Iisalmi partnership, community organisations and excluded groups are more the objects than the subjects of partnership management structures. These partnerships therefore represent partnership **'on behalf of' rather than with** excluded groups. This model of partnership may well facilitate the development of more effective partnership among the partners concerned but, as the Belgian research report points out, such partnerships cannot achieve the benefits which come through involvement and empowerment of excluded groups (Carton et al 1996).

These findings from the research add weight to the conclusions of other research by the Foundation on local community action and participation (Chanan 1992 and 1997), which has argued that policies for social cohesion at national and regional level will be more effective if they are supplemented by policies for 'micro social cohesion' at the level of localities and especially in disadvantaged areas. Local partnerships can potentially play a key role in this respect, but this will require partnerships to ensure the effective representation and active involvement of community interests and disadvantaged groups, so that their strategies promote the solidarity of local people in a broad sense, as a general objective, not just as a function of specific projects. Community representation will often require active support to be given to those voluntary and community organisations and associations which play a vital role as intermediaries between local people and policy makers.

Partnership and equal opportunity

Crosscutting such issues about the representation of the public sector, employers and trade unions and the voluntary and community sectors in local partnerships are questions of gender and equal opportunity. The research identifies several instances of local partnerships in which women are strongly represented, as in the following example.

The Women's Foundation, Steyr, arose from initiatives from a group of women trade unionists concerned at the implications for female employment of the structural crisis of local industries. The core of the partnership lies in the close collaboration between women in the trade unions, and others in public authorities with trade union backgrounds or sympathies. This 'horizontal partnership' has been successful in enlisting the active support of regional, provincial and federal authorities, and there are close working relationships on training issues with local employers and trade unions. The partnership takes the form of a Foundation, and all the members of the Executive Board are women. Within the partnership, the political and trade union skills of the participants have been important in developing effective ways of working.

More widely, women play active and prominent roles in many local partnerships, but are much more likely to be community representatives, and project leaders than partner representatives on partnership boards or management committees where policy decisions are made. This distinction reflects the fact that in most local partnerships formal and active equal opportunity policies and guidelines are conspicuous by their absence. Indeed, many of those who are involved in local partnerships do not recognise their relevance. This tends to mean that degree and level of opportunity for women within local partnerships is less than that for men: there are exceptions, but women are more often involved at lower levels, and in less powerful positions. Even when the focus of partnership is on issues such as employment for women, this does not necessarily mean that women hold the positions of leadership.

In Ireland the issue of the representation of women in partnerships is now being more seriously and openly addressed. Following a recommendation of the Second Commission on the Status of Women in Ireland, new procedures for 'gender quotas' introduced by the government (ADM 1996) now require local partnerships to ensure that at least 40% of the members of partnership management boards are women. In the Tallaght Partnership, 41% of the management committee are women, an achievement made possible by the quota recommendation and the strong local women's networks which ensured that such issues were raised. But despite this, the pursuance of equal opportunity issues is hindered by the limited numbers of women in senior positions in partner organisations. It is too early to make an overall assessment of what effect the Irish quota measure will have in practice, but if it is successful it may provide a benchmark for other countries and programmes.

This section has showed that there are wide differences in the extent to which local partnerships have succeeded in developing effective structures and processes of interest representation. On the one hand, many of those involved felt that partnership structures did indeed offer adequate representation to many key interests, expressed in comments such as 'the balance is about right' or 'all the key players are there'. This, it is clear from the research, did not normally mean that all partners had equal influence, but that their representation was considered to be proportionate to their contribution to, or stake in, the partnership. On the other hand, the research also documents very different experience, both of partnerships which have not succeeded in representing interests effectively, and cases where different partners and actors express conflicting views. (It must also be noted that the research may also give more prominence to views 'from the inside' of partnerships, and as such may tend to overlook the perspectives of interests not represented within partnerships.)

Consensus and conflict: negotiating partnership

Local partnerships must not only establish structures and processes which ensure the representation of key interests, but must negotiate a consensus around a common strategy and the consequent action plan, and managing the conflicts which are likely to arise. Building and maintaining a partnership strategy involves:

• the collaboration of unequal partners,

• with widely differing resources, expertise, culture and interests.

The Onyar Est partnership in Girona illustrates several important factors in partnership building: the way in which a partnership approach offered **new solutions to problems**; active **leadership** within the partnership; and the availability of **new resources**. In Girona, social policy initiatives by the urban authorities came at the right time to achieve success in attracting funding from the EU's Poverty 3 programme. These new resources legitimated a new approach in the city, so that when the initial partners and leading individuals approached other potential partners, many responses were positive. The partnership was able to build on this by concentrating on **practical projects and actions** in which partners could join. The reservations of some partners were, therefore, overcome by **active involvement** in partnership activity. In particular, when the partnership realised that employment actions were vital to its success, and that the focus of the partnership needed to be shifted from social issues to include economic ones, a practical basis existed for drawing the social partners into partnership. Nonetheless, despite these successes, the Girona partnership has not been able to survive the termination of the Poverty 3 programme, illustrating the fragility of partnership and the length of time needed to build it.

Two other partnerships illustrate how a **strong local identity and 'dynamic'** is an important factor in building partnership. The Okospeicher partnership in Wulkow is founded on the commitment and mobilisation of local people - in the clearly demarcated context of a small village - against the external threat posed by the proposals by public authorities to extinguish the community and resettle the population. This local mobilisation, aided by sympathetic external actors, has proved sufficiently strong for local actors to remain at the core of a cohesive partnership, while drawing in external resources and building important external links. ARCIL in central Portugal has had similar success in this respect, reflecting the very strong foundation of the partnership in **local collaborative relationships and associations** rooted in positive traditions in local society. The case study of the ARCIL partnership shows how building and maintaining an effective partnership from this base has involved **managing the tension between stability and change**: between objectives of social solidarity and a 'local enterprise' approach.

In partnerships such as the Okospeicher and ARCIL, the strength of the local community roots of the partnership has enabled the partnership to arrive at an effective working relationship between local community partners and public agencies, overcoming problems associated with the bureaucratised approach which may characterise the operation of public sector organisations. In many partnerships, however, **tensions between public agencies and community partners** has not been overcome so successfully. In the partnership in Se and S Nicolau in Porto, 'formal partnership' in which the dominant role is played by public agencies has not been paralleled by effective 'informal partnership' with community organisations and excluded groups.

Several of the case studies highlight **the role of local politicians**. In some cases, local elected representatives may be unable to reach agreement among themselves, or to find an accommodation between their political objectives and the agenda of partnership. Short-term influences such as **political turbulence** and change resulting from elections can hinder the implementation of an agreed programme. Such partnerships become forums for conflict not consensus. Factors such as these, along with the limited functions of local authorities, explain why local politicians are not included in some partnerships. The research shows, however, that local politicians can also play **key leadership roles** in local partnerships, reflecting their democratic responsibility for the local community, and bringing greater legitimacy to partnerships. In Girona and North Tyneside local politicians played such a leadership role. In Coventry and Warwickshire in England, an important basis for the formation of the partnership was a new spirit of collaboration among politicians from neighbouring local authorities which had not previously worked very closely together.

A few of the partnerships in the research illustrate **more comprehensive obstacles** to establishing effective partnership. This is particularly the case in certain countries, although it is not a problem confined to them. In Greece, because of **negative cultural and attitudinal factors,** none of the three partnerships for which case studies were conducted show success in establishing durable partnership relationships at the local level, a situation encapsulated by the comments of the Greek research study on the partnership oriented to the needs of the Muslim majority:

"It was impossible to create permanent, stable and flexible partnerships because of the variety of economic, social, behavioural and attitudinal problems and aspirations".

In Spain, the partnership initiatives in El Ribeiro in Galicia and in the Basque country have so far not succeeded in establishing a working structure of partnership. In El Ribeiro this is attributed to four factors:

1. the absence of strong associative conditions in local society;

2. the lack of collaboration between different levels of public administration and different state agencies;

3. the complex framework and structure of partnership proposed; and

4. the short timescale within which the initiative had to achieve results. The last point contrasts sharply with the experience of many of the more successful partnerships analysed in the research. In the ARCIL partnership for example the **slow and patient nature of the process of negotiating partnership** is strongly emphasised.

In summary therefore, the research highlights a number of factors which assist in building partnership. These include:

- clear identification of the benefits to be gained;

- strong leadership;

- a strong local identity and dynamic;

- active involvement of partners in the shaping and implementation of strategy;

- seeing new solutions to problems;

- co-operating to obtain new resources.

But building partnership needs time and patience. It is difficult in negative cultural and attitudinal environments of :

- local political turbulence;

- absence of a strong local associative tradition;

- lack of a collaborative tradition in the public sector.

Working methods

Local partnerships must not only negotiate and maintain clear and agreed strategies but must implement these through action programmes and projects. The research shows that this requires partnership at a different - operational - level, and a different set of skills and aptitudes. The research indicates that effective operation will depend not only on the working methods of the partnerships themselves, and particularly their project teams, and to an extent on the capacities of individuals, but also on the relationships between the partnership, partner organisations and other key external actors.

Modes of operation

The wide variation in the size, scope and resources of local partnerships means that there are few simple answers to questions about what constitute effective partnership working methods for implementing programmes and projects. At one end of the spectrum, some small partnerships such as those in Wulkow and Wedding in Germany for example exhibit relatively simple and informal - but robust and flexible - structures and working processes. There is a high degree of interaction between, and commitment by, all those involved in the partnership at the operational level. The evidence suggests that this model (which we might call 'direct' or 'face to face' or 'micro-partnership') can work very effectively, particularly in small and defined geographical areas and communities. Most partnerships are however larger and more complex than this, and direct partnership communication can be only one part of the answer to the search for effective working methods.

Some of the most challenging operational issues confront the larger, multidimensional partnerships, such as those funded by EU programmes and national government programmes such as City Challenge, and especially those relying on several programmes for their funding. In these cases, partnerships need to combine high levels of organisation and management with flexibility and innovation. While these partnerships have often been able to draw on guidelines provided by national and European programmes, these have sometimes been found constraining rather than enabling, denying partnerships flexibility to respond to changing circumstances and needs, and imposing considerable bureaucratic demands. These large and complex partnerships have had to develop **sophisticated organisational structures** to facilitate their work.

The Paul Partnership in Limerick, for example, developed a highly complex management structure analogous in many ways to that of a substantial firm or public agency. The main management committee/board of directors of 24 directors nominated by 16 partner organisations meets every six weeks on average to make the main policy and funding decisions. Beneath the management committee are three sub-tiers: three operational subcommittees, six programme development workshops and three special project committees. These enable up to 200 people to have positions within the partnership, thus widening the representation of partners. The partnership project team employs 50 full-time and part-time staff, and itself has a multi-tier structure, with a director, a three person management team, project staff working on specific project areas, and a fourth level of staff on temporary projects and placements. The partnership's action plan includes 21 discrete activity areas organised in six broad groups, and while some activities are designed and implemented by the partnership itself, others, such as a network of community action centres are managed externally, especially by partner organisations.

There is however always a potential for such structures to become over-elaborate, to the detriment of strategic direction or operational effectiveness, and putting at risk some of the essentials of the partnership approach. In the Paul Partnership, criticisms of bureaucratism have been made by some partners, and addressing these is now one of the challenges facing the partnership.

An effective response to the implementation of complex and multidimensional programmes may lie in the establishment **of subcommittees, working groups or similar mechanisms**, each of which take responsibility for a particular aspect of the partnership's work. This is of course a fairly standard organisational approach, but the research shows that it can be adapted effectively within an inter-organisational, partnership context.

Local partnerships also employ different modes of operation in implementing their strategies and action plans. These can include both a **delivery** function (the direct implementation of programmes and projects), and a **brokerage** role (mediating between funding programmes and external actors and the deliverers of actions, including partner organisations). In some partnerships, the delivery function is very dominant, especially when the partnership has been formed in response to the requirements of a specific programme. Examples are the Lille

City Contract and North Tyneside City Challenge partnerships. In extreme cases, partnerships of this sort may be in danger of becoming simply no more than delivery structures in which other benefits of partnership become dissipated or lost. As one partner in the Coventry and Warwickshire partnership in England commented:

"The danger is that we are merely reproducing the local authority".

In other partnerships, the brokerage role is dominant. This is the case in two very different Austrian partnerships. The Social and Health Care Districts partnership in the Tyrol fulfils a networking and brokerage role between social care professionals, voluntary organisations and local community interests aimed at providing a more integrated and cost effective approach in social services provision. The Carinthian Labour Foundation Programme, a partnership framework between the regional employment service and the social partners, promotes the establishment of labour foundations which offer comprehensive and targeted packages of labour market measures in specific industrial sectors affected by economic change and restructuring. Many partnerships, of course, combine elements of both modes of working.

Project teams

In most of the partnerships analysed in the research, the establishment of a project team within the partnership structure has been adopted as the main means of operationalising the partnership strategy and implementing the programme and individual projects. In general, this has been a successful mechanism. A high proportion of the case studies identify the contribution of the project team as one of the principal factors influencing success. There are a number of different dimensions to this role:

- The project team can play an important role in building the partnership itself, taking action to draw in partners, consolidate partnership relationships, and obtain funding.

- Project teams can also play crucial roles in building stronger relationships between the partnership and local communities, especially as in most instances the partner representatives on partnership boards tend to sit in a part-time capacity and it is the project team which represents the reservoir of full-time, committed personnel on which the partnership can draw.

- Most importantly, project teams play central roles in implementing partnership strategies and activity programmes, either directly (where the partnership operates in an agency mode) or in collaboration with partner organisations and other bodies when the partnership operates by brokerage methods.

In some cases, partnerships have built up substantial staff complements. The Paul Partnership, it was noted above, has a project team of 50. ARCIL employs 97 full and part-time staff. However, these examples are the exception not the rule, and many partnerships, including those delivering European and national programmes, operate with quite small project teams. This 'lean' model sometimes relies on substantial support from key partners, as for example in the Western Isles and Skye and Lochalsh LEADER partnership, where the Local Enterprise Companies provided substantial staffing support particularly at the technical, project level. Where partnerships do not have substantial programme funding, small project teams may confront very substantial and wide-ranging responsibilities. Several of the case studies, such as that of the Coventry and Warwickshire partnership, have reported the views of those involved that more staff resources are necessary to support the core activities and running of partnerships.

Project teams have often been able to recruit individuals with a considerable commitment to the partnership's objectives, and with a range of skills. Their members have often displayed a considerable ability to innovate within local partnership structures which has avoided some of the constraints of more established and bureaucratic organisations. The recent OECD study of Irish partnerships compares local partnership project teams with the 'flexible workteam' model characteristic of leading edge private sector firms. However, against these advantages, project teams appear to have frequently suffered from high staff turnover associated with the temporary nature of funding and staffing, and in some instances levels of remuneration are low. It should not be the case that commitment to working in local partnerships which are seeking innovative solutions to problems of unemployment and social exclusion is at the cost of job security and conditions of employment.

Key individuals

As well as the key role played by project teams, a significant number of the case studies of local partnerships identify the critical contribution made by key individuals. These are sometimes leaders of project teams, but may also be leading partners and members of partnership boards and management committees. This reflects the 'networking' dimension of partnership and the importance of individuals who are able to cross organisational boundaries and build bridges between organisations and individuals with different cultures and ways of working. The key individual may be one who can bridge the divide between the local community and organisational partners, from the basis of a knowledge of both 'worlds'. Such individual(s) may also possess the capacity to formulate the partnership's 'mission' and strategy and 'convert' doubters and critical partners to active participation in the partnership. Both professionals and politicians may be able to play these roles.

However, an over-reliance on such individuals can be a weakening factor in the long term, given the difficulty of sustaining achievements following the departure of a key actor, and the fact that the contribution required from such individuals may change at different stages of a partnership's life, particularly as it moves from the initial construction of a partnership alliance and the acquisition of resources to the implementation and evaluation/monitoring of a programme and projects. Local partnerships should avoid staff who, as the French research report suggests,

"find themselves at the heart of a partnership for the wrong reasons: to satisfy their acute obsession with the culture of meetings, to enjoy congenial contacts with a range of very diverse partners, to give the impression of causing a stir......(and who flourish in a context of)....opaqueness of initiatives and confusion about objectives" (Le Gales and Loncle, 1996).

External links and communication

Good communications are vital to local partnerships. In the first place, partnerships need to be able to influence the actions of partner organisations. This requires the development of effective mechanisms of communication **for reporting and feedback** from the representatives of partners to their organisations or 'constituencies'. In general, the findings from the research show that this is an issue which has been given relatively little attention by many partnerships. Representatives are often chosen or nominated to a partnership body on an individual basis, and it may not be clear whether they are delegates who must refer back to their organisations for decisions, or are mandated to take decisions on behalf of their organisation. In many cases, in the words of the Belgian research, partnerships exhibit 'soft' forms of representation in which there are no, or only informal, procedures or requirements for reporting back. The local partnerships in North Tyneside and Coventry and Warwickshire in the UK, illustrate the differences in practice in this respect between public authorities and community representatives, who frequently do have formal reporting back systems, and other partners, such as employers and trade unions, where such mechanisms are much less widespread. In the UK, local authorities are now giving greater priority to the consideration of partnership issues by council committees, buttressed by clearer requirements for officers and elected representatives to report back. A few partnerships, such as the Women's Foundation, Steyr, and the Carinthian Labour Foundation Programme in Austria offer valuable examples of good practice by the social partners in this respect. In the Steyr Women's Foundation, communication is made easier by the existence of an Advisory Council for the local partnership, which includes representatives of women trade unionists from national, provincial and regional levels. However, in some partnerships the individual nature of the representation of employers and employer organisations tends to mean that there is limited feedback either to the individual's employer or to organisations representing the employer interest. The strength (or weakness) of institutions, such as chambers of commerce and industry, representing local employers and businesses, is an important factor in this respect. In Ireland, where local partnerships are becoming an increasingly important complement to mainstream policies, it is recognised that clearer and stronger lines of communication are needed, both to ensure that individuals serving as representatives on partnerships are able to represent their parent organisation effectively, and, vice versa, to assist partner organisations to review and adapt their own policies and practices in the light of agreed partnership strategies.

Local partnerships also need good **'vertical' lines of communication** with national and European policymakers. Many local partnerships have cultivated such links in the course of the implementation of programmes supported by national and EU funds. However the experience of partnerships such as the Se and S Nicolau partnership in Porto, and the Western Isles and Skye and Lochalsh LEADER partnership reflects the research's findings that the regulations and financial procedures through which resources are delivered from European and national programmes to local partnerships can sometimes be inflexible and at odds with local needs. Local partnerships often therefore have to devote time to lobbying and informing in order to try to bridge the gap between programmes and local needs.

A number of the case studies, such as those of the Paul and Tallaght Partnerships in Ireland, show how partnerships which have given priority to effective links with national and European policymakers have had considerable success in securing new funding, and in influencing new policy initiatives by national government.

The research also highlights the difficulty faced by many partnerships in **communicating 'horizontally'** with other similar partnerships, whether this be within specific programmes; within countries, or transnationally within the EU.

Too often the framework for learning from local practice is too uni-directional, with information flowing from the local level to 'higher' levels, rather than disseminated multi-directionally on a networking principle. While most EU programmes have allocated some resources to transnational exchange between local partnerships, the research suggests that this has seldom been adequate, and also that too often the agendas for such exchanges have been those of the managers of the programmes, rather than those directly involved in local partnerships. The importance of transnational and other exchange lies both in the innovative nature of many local partnerships, and the consequent need to exchange experience with other innovators , establish 'benchmarks' of achievement, and the need to avoid waste of resources through a fragmented localised learning process which 'reinvents the wheel' in each locality. Examples of what can be achieved are illustrated by the IN LOCO partnership in Portugal, and the local partnerships in Wedding and Wulkow in Germany. Prominent actors in these partnerships have been active in establishing transnational networks among community-led local development initiatives, enabling individual projects to learn from the experience of others. The Wedding and Wulkow partnerships participate in a European Network for Self-Help and Local Development, which has organised three major European conferences for the exchange of practice and research among grassroots initiatives (Bauhaus Dessau Foundation 1996).

Skills and training

Working in partnership requires specific skills and expertise to facilitate effective operation. The priority may be for professional skills in the main activity areas, such as, for example, social services provision or local economic and community development. In other cases, the need may be for management skills, including interpersonal and networking abilities, but also skills in project and personnel management and accounting and financial control.

The Portuguese research describes how ARCIL and other local partnerships have created *communities of experts*, drawing together professionals with a range of skills from different partners, arguing that

"the creation and maintenance of a community of experts requires the constant updating of dialogue skills and their enrichment through ongoing training in communication. ARCIL has taken significant steps towards stimulating these dialogue skills" (Rodrigues and Stoer, 74-75).

The Belgian research shows how the BRUTEC partnership in Brussels brought together the complementary knowledge and contributions of different partners. The partnership combined the innovatory experience of three training centres in developing training approaches appropriate to excluded groups, the experience of the social partners in what is required for the 'real world' of work', and the financial resources and political skills of public authorities. The research points to the kind of skills this requires from all partners: *respect* for the autonomy of each partner; *impartiality*, so that each partner is treated equally; *co-operation* and *sharing* of experience; and the systematic circulation of information. In addition, the Belgian research points to partnership requiring both 'skills and passion' - in the sense of a **commitment** by all partners and by those working for the partnership to the objectives of tackling unemployment, poverty and exclusion. The national report for Germany shows how, in all of the three case studies in Wedding, Wulkow and Dortmund, a very important factor in success was a capacity to combine the contributions of local and external 'partners'. Thus the partnership in Wulkow, while rooted in the needs, and the contributions, of local people, did not hesitate to draw on the contributions of outside experts from universities and other institutes. In Wedding, a variety of formal and informal working groups within the partnership mobilised skills and knowledge, locally and from outside the local community. In the partnerships in Mantes and Brittany (GALCOB) in France, the research shows, similarly, how professional teams within the partnerships were able both to create effective working relationships across organisational boundaries, and, in some cases, to create effective links with social groups and local associations. In both these cases, this dimension of local partnership, taking the form of a 'community of experts' including both the expertise of professionals and the knowledge of local people, proved successful.

In some cases, such as some of the Irish partnerships, local partnerships can draw on secondments from partner agencies for some skills. In some cases this can work very successfully, but the research suggests that this kind of arrangement can sometimes suffer from a lack of full commitment on the part of seconding partners and the individuals concerned to the partnership, and inequalities (eg of pay and terms of employment contract) within the partnership between seconded and other staff.

The conclusions drawn from these issues in the research studies point to the need for more substantial resourcing of training and development for those involved in local partnerships, including the staff of partnership project teams. Where partnership employment is reaching substantial dimensions within a Member State, national studies point to the need to consider the implication of the emergence of a new sector and type of employment in terms of its conditions, training and other needs.

Resources

As discussed earlier in this chapter, the acquisition of new resources, most typically from a European or national programme, is frequently a focus around which partnerships seek to negotiate a consensual strategy. However the research also highlights the crucial resource issues which arise for local partnerships at a later stage, when they need to seek further sources of funding in order to maintain the continuity of their activity. Local partnerships may be able to draw on internally generated income, from partners or from project activity, to help to provide a continuing resource base, but in most cases partnerships will need to access further sources of external funding.

In some of the case studies, such as Onyar Est in Girona, the local partnership was not successful in attracting further funding when the initial funds (from the Poverty 3 programme) came to an end, and this has meant that many of the advances made have not been sustained. The Paul Partnership in Limerick, in contrast, has been very successful in diversifying this funding base by accessing further funding from a wide range of national and EU sources. This has been achieved partly through the development of close relationships with national and European policymakers, to whom the partnership was able to demonstrate considerable initial achievements. During the period 1990-1995 the Paul Partnership received financial resources from no fewer than nine different sources of national and EU funding. But the cost to the partnership of dependence on a changing resource base has been a need to cope with constantly changing requirements of different funding programmes, necessitating some modification of the partnership's objectives, changes in the pattern of partner representation, and the emergence of very complicated structures and procedures. Despite very careful management, this has led to some lack of clarity of direction and criticisms of bureaucratic cumbersomeness. These problems are indicative of the dangers which local partnerships face of becoming 'funding driven' to the detriment of the implementation of a consistent strategy.

Conclusion

The research shows that building and maintaining a successful alliance among partners is a difficult balancing act. It involves difficult processes of:

- negotiation and communication;

- bringing together the appropriate partners;

- building a durable alliance between them around a consensual strategy;

- putting in place the necessary organisational structures and procedures to implement an action plan;

- finding the skills and resources needed;

- establishing effective links at the local, national and transnational levels.

Not all partnerships have succeeded in these respects. Several of the national reports, such as that for Spain, highlight the high 'death rate' of local partnership initiatives. The research has, on the whole, concentrated on examples of partnerships which have achieved some stability and progress, and so it probably understates the extent to which other partnership initiatives have failed to get off the ground or survive. However where local partnerships have been successfully developed they have been able to demonstrate positive impacts, as the next chapter shows.

Chapter 6

The Impact of Local Partnerships

Introduction

This chapter presents the evidence from the research concerning the achievements of local partnerships. There are several dimensions to these:

- Issues concerning the **evaluation** of the impact of partnerships.

- The impact of partnership on the **policy process:**

  a) the impact of partnership as a **working method** offering better ways of formulating and delivering policies at the local level;

  b) the impact of the local partnership approach on the **wider policy process.**

- The impact on policy **outcomes**: in this context, on the problems of unemployment, poverty and exclusion which the local partnerships have sought to combat.

Evaluating the impact of local partnerships

Evaluating the impact of local partnerships is recognised by the European Commission as a challenging task (Monnier 1997). It requires forms of evaluation which are adapted to the pluralistic nature of partnership. Evaluation of partnerships needs to be conducted collaboratively, reflecting and respecting differences in objectives and expectations among different interests, as well as commonly defined goals. Because the nature of partnerships is so often a matter of negotiation and compromise, formal evaluation procedures developed in more simple situations may not work well. Nonetheless, detailed analysis of impacts is essential to guide and consolidate the partnership process and to ensure the achievement of goals and the effective use of financial and other resources.

Evaluation of the impact of local partnerships on problems of unemployment, poverty and social exclusion raises difficult questions. How far does the achievement of specific, quantifiable, but often limited targets, contribute to the reduction of poverty, deprivation and exclusion? Have partnerships been able to reach the most marginalised and excluded social groups? Where significant sums of money have been spent, has value been achieved?

Where the gains of partnership are seen in terms of process rather than product, what are the measures of success? To what extent can the achievements of local partnerships be attributed to partnership working, not merely to the programmes which they have implemented and the resources which they have deployed? How can evaluation include not only the impact on the local area, but wider impacts?

In assessing impact, the research has, first, drawn on existing monitoring and evaluation undertaken by or for the local partnerships. In some of them, especially those where significant financial resources have been deployed, objectives and targets have been precisely specified, in terms of employment created or protected for example, or 'leverage' of additional resources, and monitoring and evaluation procedures have sought to measure concrete progress in achieving such targets. Partnerships such as North Tyneside City Challenge and BRUTEC prepare annual progress reports of activity undertaken and outcomes of projects. Those which participated in the Poverty 3 programme, and a number of others with more limited financial resources, have placed more emphasis on evaluating the achievements of partnership in changing the attitudes and activities of partner agencies; and in initiating processes of community involvement and empowerment. Evaluation has tended to be of a 'formative' nature, with more emphasis on the contribution of monitoring and evaluation to the ongoing work of the partnership than on assessing outcomes and impacts post-hoc.

Other local partnerships however have undertaken little or no evaluation. The LEADER I programme for example did not require local partnerships to undertake a systematic evaluation of their job creation impact, which often cannot therefore be quantified, although some individual LEADER partnerships, such as that in the Western Isles and Skye and Lochalsh, did commission their own evaluations. This confirms that, as local partnerships become more widespread, the development of more rigorous procedures for monitoring and evaluation of impacts and outcomes, particularly of the benefits and costs of partnership working, should be a priority. The research study for Ireland, where there has been extensive evaluation of some, though not all, local partnerships, highlights the contribution which independent evaluators can make to the assessment of the impacts and outcomes of partnerships, and to the dissemination of good practice (Walsh et al 1997).

This research project has not had the resources to be able to undertake detailed empirical evaluations of the outcomes or impacts of the local partnerships, although it has drawn on such studies where they already exist. It has, however, contributed to the evaluation of impacts through the detailed qualitative case studies undertaken, and through the 'stakeholder' methodology adopted, involving interviews with local partners and others. The study is therefore able to present information on the views of different actors and interests about the impact of local partnerships. In particular, the project has tried to identify the benefits and costs of partnership working itself, as well as that of the programmes and projects delivered by the partnerships. This provides some important evidence of the positive impacts which partnerships can have, as well as some of the limits to what has been, and can be, achieved by the local partnership approach.

The impact of local partnership on the policy process

a) The impact of local partnership as a working method

The research shows clearly that the process of partnership working can lead to important improvements in the processes of policy formulation and implementation at the local level. Synthesising the different experiences of the case studies, the research suggests that the impact of partnership working can be summed up in terms of three key concepts, which encapsulate both the advantages of partnership but also some of the challenges which it poses. These are:

* the **co-ordination** of the policies and programmes of key actors

* the **integration** of different strands of activity within a partnership strategy and action plan

* a capacity to produce **synergy and innovation.**

Policy co-ordination
Policy co-ordination refers to the way in which a partnership framework can help to ensure that the activities of different partner organisations work to a

common purpose, even if remaining under separate control. The co-ordination of policies of partner organisations can often be the initial form of benefit from partnership. For example, in the partnership in Coventry and Warwickshire in the United Kingdom, the initial consolidation of the partnership was greatly enhanced by the perceived benefits to all partners of being able to co-ordinate policies across institutional local authority boundaries, enabling the scale of policy initiative to coincide much more closely with the reality of the local economy. This brought benefits both to the local authorities themselves, especially in the form of better co-ordination between the main town, Coventry, and the surrounding area, Warwickshire, and between them and smaller district authorities. Other members of the partnership, such as the local Training and Enterprise Council, and businesses, also recognised the benefits of collaboration at a subregional level. Similar gains from co-ordination between partners are evident, for example, in the Hanko partnership in Finland. Here the partnership has provided a forum for better co-ordination of policies towards youth and crime, between departments in the municipality (social services; sports, leisure and culture, education), the police, local health and employment centres, and parish representatives.

Local partnership can thus lead to the building of a stronger local 'policy community' in which local policymakers interact more effectively and coherently together in tackling problems of social exclusion, both by strengthening contacts between partners who already had responsibilities in this respect, but also by involving new actors, such as the social partners and local associations and groups. This is, however, a more challenging task in some contexts than others. Several case studies, such as those of the partnerships in Wulkow and the Western Isles and Skye and Lochalsh, and the LEDA study (Humphreys 1996), note the advantages which partnerships seem to derive in relatively small and homogeneous geographical areas, and among a restricted range of partners. While there are good examples of larger well functioning partnerships, the research also offers more cautionary examples of over-ambitious attempts to build broader partnerships which have encountered difficulties. The attempt to build a partnership basis for a multidimensional strategy against poverty in the Basque country was probably conducted at too ambitious a scale, and allowed too little time to build a functioning 'policy community'.

The integration of policies and actions

In some of the case studies, partnership working did not go beyond the stage of 'joint working' between actors and agencies pursuing independent activity programmes. This may well offer important benefits, but policy co-ordination of this nature may also prepare the ground for further dimensions of collaboration. The research has identified a stronger meaning to partnership, involving the pooling of resources in a common, integrated action plan 'owned' and controlled by the local partnership not by separate social actors. One of the key elements in the working definition of local partnerships adopted in the research is the existence of a formal structure of partnership independent of the partner organisations themselves, providing a basis for such an integrated action plan. This function of partnership as integration can be seen in many of the case studies, especially but not exclusively those funded by national or EU programmes, eg the City Challenge partnership in North Tyneside, and the Contrat du Plan partnership in Lille which are implementing large and complex regeneration programmes.

The development of such an independent, integrated action plan can generate several crucial **advantages**:

• It facilitates the creation of a **multidimensional response** to problems which cannot be solved on a single issue/policy basis. In particular, the integration of economic and social dimensions of action against exclusion, and the agencies responsible, can be a major gain of partnership. Leading figures in the partnership in Onyar Est, Girona, for example, worked hard to ensure that economic development and labour market policies were integrated into the partnership's activity, realising that otherwise socially-oriented actions would have much less impact on poverty and exclusion. In the Poverty 3 partnership in Mantes however political disagreements led to the implementation of a disaggregated bundle of initiatives rather than an integrated multidimensional response.

• The development of an integrated action plan enables partnerships to draw together, and thus draw upon, the **knowledge, skills and resources** of different partners. In some partnerships, this may mean bringing together the **social goods and skills** produced by the public sector with the **business methods and skills of** the private sector, for example in promoting entrepreneurship in rural areas as LEADER partnerships have done, or in linking training programmes more effectively to jobs, as the BRUTEC partnership in Brussels has done. The ARCIL project in Portugal shows how the integration of public, not-for-profit and community cultures and resources can be brought about to the benefit of a disadvantaged group, those with disabilities. The IN LOCO partnership, also in Portugal, tackled some of the difficult questions which the integration of different perspectives poses for partnerships' strategies. As a local socio-economic development partnership, IN LOCO has had to confront both the tensions which often exist between grassroots organisations and public sector bodies, and the strategic choices between a 'modernising', 'enterprise' approach and one more rooted in local traditions of social solidarity. In both these cases, a primary factor in the ability of the partnership to integrate the contributions of different sectors was the central role played by a strong voluntary organisation, rooted in the local community, and influential individuals able to bring public, private and community interests together.

- Local partnerships can also prove effective frameworks for the **vertical integration** of national, regional and local policies and initiatives. This advantage of partnership is particularly important in increasing the coherence and effectiveness of public policies. Case studies such as those of the Women's Foundation Steyr and the Carinthian Labour Foundation Programme in Austria show that partnerships can also enable interventions by the social partners at national and regional level to be targeted effectively on those localities where they are most needed.

- The integration of different resources can increase the **viability of initiatives and projects**, as in the Ökospeicher in Wulkow, where the involvement of a wide range of interests created an ability to develop joint projects, find funding for them and bring together partners to implement them. Integration within an agreed partnership framework can prevent policy and agency conflict and competition, as in the WISL LEADER partnership where, before the advent of the partnership, relations between local authorities and the Local Enterprise Companies had been distant, lacking in trust and characterised by competition over responsibility for local economic development.

However, the effective integration of the contributions of different partners undoubtedly poses a number of **challenges** to local partnerships and to national and European programmes involving a local partnership approach.

- It can involve significant **transaction costs**. These are the time and resources that need to be spent in building partnership relationships, implementing programmes and projects jointly, and ensuring good communications among those involved. These can be substantial, especially in cases where partnerships are very broad either in terms of their strategy or their partner mix, as in the Coventry and Warwickshire or the Paul Partnerships, or when partnership ways of working are very poorly understood, as in El Ribeiro in Spain. For many partner organisations, costs can be counted in terms of both money and the time commitment of often senior and experienced staff. The demands of partnership can bear particularly heavily on community organisations and the representatives of excluded groups and communities. The Paul Partnership is one of those which have made a considerable investment in community development to assist community interests in sharing in partnership decision making and its benefits.

- If dangers of divided and unclear responsibility within partnerships are to be avoided, there needs to be **clear allocation of responsibilities**. This may mean agreement within the partnership on who is the 'lead' partner. In the North Tyneside City Challenge partnership for example, the local authority provides the financial and accounting resources which are crucial for a partnership delivering a multi-million ECU programme. Clear allocation of responsibilities may also, as in the Se and S Nicolau partnership in Porto, be achieved through explicit contractual arrangements between partners.

- Linked to the issue of clear responsibility is the challenge of **accountability**. In the Irish case, this issue is posed particularly sharply by the rapid and widespread permeation of the local partnership approach in local development strategies. This has highlighted the way in which, while the autonomy of local partnerships from mainstream administrative structures has been important in enabling them to develop new approaches to problems, the consequence is now that key areas of local policy are distanced from electoral democratic accountability. A similar problem exists, albeit in a less acute form, in other countries. Moreover, while the representation of community interests on partnerships' boards undoubtedly assists in making them directly accountable to local communities, this in turn places greater weight on the extent to which community 'partners' are representative of, and accountable to, the communities themselves. The question of accountability also needs to be posed in relation to other partners such as employers or trade union representatives - to whom are they accountable for the actions of local partnerships of which they are active members, and for the expenditure of public money?

- Several national research studies emphasise that partnerships need to develop a culture which respects the **diversity** of partners' contributions. The challenge here is that the integration of different activities within a partnership framework may erode the individuality of partners' con-tributions, especially perhaps where the partnership is formed around a large funded programme, as in the cases of the French Contrat de Ville and the UK City Challenge partnerships, which dominates the partnership's activity and approach, so that partners are in danger of being reduced to delivery organisations. Integration should not mean homogenisation. This may be a particular danger for smaller voluntary and community organisations which, as the assessment of the Lille City Contract partnership suggests, may find themselves submerged in partnership programmes by more powerful partners.

- Maintaining the diversity of partners' contributions within partnerships will be easier when it is apparent that all partners are prepared to be **flexible**. It will be less easy when this is not the case with some partners. Case studies in Greece, Ireland, Spain and other countries have identified a lack of flexibility on the part of national state agencies as a significant challenge to be overcome in many partnerships.

- Finally, the substantial **timescale** necessary to firmly root processes of partnership working among partner organisations represents a considerable challenge to many partnerships. It is not surprising to find that in some of the more recent initiatives researched, such as that in Coventry and Warwickshire, partners feel that it is 'too soon to judge' the value of the partnership. However similar perspectives are also found in some of the more established and, on many counts, more successful local partnerships. The Paul Partnership in Limerick still considers itself to be in a developmental phase, despite having been in existence since 1990 and with a successful track record of attracting funding from a variety of sources over the period. There are clear implications here for the timescale within which local partnerships can be expected to have an impact, and this will be discussed further below.

Synergy and innovation

Where partnerships succeed in integrating the contributions of different partners, and promoting positive change in their practices, this will produce benefits from partnership working which may be defined in terms of synergy and innovation. These may be of two main kinds:

- **Resource synergy** is the combination of partner contributions to produce more than the sum of the parts, including levering in further financial contributions to projects, both from local partners but also from outside the local area, and gaining better value for money from resource inputs through their integration in an agreed strategy and action plan. A number of examples of this have already been identified. It must be noted though that this may only be 'local synergy', not a resource gain at the wider level, if the partnership has merely attracted resources that would otherwise have gone to another location. The basis of funding in the LEADER partnerships appeared to be particularly effective in producing resource synergy, because its distribution and use was not determined a priori but was available as a flexible resource for the partnership to use to stimulate local initiative. This principle appears to deserve much wider application

• Local partnerships can provide an institutional framework for **policy innovation**. Thus the recent OECD study of local partnerships in Ireland (Sabel, 1996), identifies them as key catalysts of innovation, with a potential both to introduce a new and more proactive attitude to local economic development within the public sector, and also to introduce change in the local economy itself. In the UK, partnerships have been promoted by government as means of promoting innovation, especially perhaps by changing the attitudes and practices of local government. Local LEADER partnerships have produced new thinking in rural development, both among policy makers and by changing the attitudes to development of local people and communities, although the case studies in South Kerry and Brittany suggest that such changed attitudes may still be confined to local elites rather than the population at large. The research studies for Finland and Germany identify problems of centralisation and bureaucratisation in social policy, and underline the potential of local partnership to produce policy innovation and to respond to problems of exclusion that national policies seem unable to address on their own. The Greek research report proposes that local partnership might come to play a catalytic role in a more effective response to problems of poverty and exclusion in that country if its potential could be more widely recognised (Robolis et al, 1996).

• An innovative role for local partnerships should be seen as **complementary** to mainstream policies, providing a more effective focus on local issues, groups, and areas, and combining the 'experiential' knowledge of local people with the 'expert' knowledge of policymakers and professionals. Individual case studies show how partnerships can be particularly effective in tackling dimensions of social exclusion, such as youth unemployment and crime in the case of the Iisalmi partnership in Finland, which transcend not only the boundaries of individual state agencies, but the boundaries between state, and civil society.

Some of the statements made by those involved in the ARCIL partnership in Portugal show that partners recognise the positive impact of partnership on the policy process:

"it is the beginning of a culture of collaboration"

"partnership promotes the best use of resources and co-responsibility for funds"

"we can do different things in the same space"

"with this dynamic, it is guaranteed that everyone will give each other feedback on what they are doing"

b) The wider policy impact of local partnerships

If the advantages of the local partnership approach are to be fully realised, then there needs to be a concern not only with the local impact which partnerships can have, but with the **diffusion and dissemination** of the best of local experience, to maximise the **dynamic** impact of local partnerships on the wider policy environment. The research illustrates how such wider dissemination of local experience can bring benefits, and also some of the barriers which need to be addressed to enable this to happen more systematically.

The Ökospeicher partnership in Wulkow, Germany, provides an example of the way in which small, local and resource constrained local partnerships may have a much wider impact if their principles can be diffused **horizontally** among other localities. In the case of the Ökospeicher, the innovative and effective nature of the initiative has attracted external recognition and resourcing which has been used by the partnership to begin to create further local initiatives on a similar model in other countries.

The IN LOCO partnership in Portugal has played an active role in the establishment of national and transnational local economic development networks to exchange experience between local initiatives.

The international awards received by the partnerships in *Hanko* and *Iisalmi in* Finland have helped to draw the attention of policymakers to their achievements.

The GALCOB partnership in Brittany stands out in the research as one which has developed an active **publicity** strategy. This was both in order to publicise the local development opportunities available from LEADER funding, because it was recognised that it was important to enhance the local identity of the area, and also as a means of lobbying for further resources. This strategy had a marked effect in raising the partnership's profile with policy makers in the region and beyond, contributing to the attraction of new funding from a government programme for local development in the area.

The *Paul Partnership* in Limerick, Ireland, has evolved to become a significant force in tackling social exclusion in the city. But in addition the Paul Partnership has had a significant influence within Ireland in heightening awareness of social exclusion, and has had an impact on mainstream national policies and programmes, through the local partnership's experience of the impact of certain local labour market policies and its work on consumer credit and debt. This kind of *vertical impact* of local partnership is encouraged in Ireland by the commitment to partnership principles in national policy, and the close relationships developed between EU and government policy directions and programmes.

However, even in the Irish case, it is recognised that a more proactive approach is needed to disseminate good practice, both horizontally between localities and vertically between local partnerships, national and EU policies and programmes, and other partners, especially employers and trade unions, at national and European levels. While EU programmes undoubtedly have provided some opportunity for transnational exchange, the research shows that many local partnerships have found it difficult to make effective use of the opportunities for transnational networking within EU programmes. This is partly because identifying what transfers well, or what knowledge is most relevant, is often very difficult. But other reasons include the costs to local partnerships of transnational (or even national) meetings, both in money terms and in staff time; the difficulties of establishing effective transnational links in the short timescale of most programmes; and the feeling of local actors that the agenda of transnational meetings tended to be controlled in a top-down fashion. There is even less opportunity currently in the majority of Member States for effective sharing of experience and learning between local partnerships participating in different programmes at EU, national and local and grassroots levels.

If good practice is not diffused effectively, then the local partnership approach may lead to **policy fragmentation,** with the benefits only accruing to those particular areas which have been successful in first securing resources from national and European programmes, and then making good use of them.

The impact of local partnerships on unemployment, poverty and social exclusion

Partnership, though, is not an end in itself, but a means of contributing to solutions to the pressing problems of unemployment, poverty and social exclusion. What light does the research shed on this crucial question for both policymakers involved in EU and national programmes and for all those involved in local partnerships?

Chapter 4 described the different aspects and dimensions of poverty and social exclusion with which local partnerships are concerned. It showed, first, that while some have broad, multidimensional strategies and action plans to combat poverty and exclusion (in both urban and rural contexts), others focus on more specific issues. These latter include two broad categories, those focusing on unemployment, employment and economic development, and those concerned with aspects of social service provision, including housing, and with community development. These distinctions will be used here in discussing the impact of the partnerships.

a) Impacts on employment and local economic development

The impact of the local partnerships on employment and economic development varied very considerably. A number of the partnerships have been able to demonstrate that they have made a considerable contribution to local job creation. The Wedding partnership in a deprived neighbourhood of Berlin has developed projects, secured resources for them and brought together partners to implement them, resulting in 90 jobs for this disadvantaged community. ARCIL in Portugal has created 200 jobs in a wide range of small local enterprises and projects set up for those with disabilities. The Carinthia Labour Foundations programme has resulted in the establishment of targeted packages of training and labour market support in towns and economic sectors where the impact of industrial change has created major employment problems. The North Tyneside City Challenge partnership claims to have created over 1,000 jobs in an area of high and long-term unemployment in the first two years of its operation, and to have helped to keep another 1500 in being. Despite this however, unemployment in the area has continued to rise as a result of the closure of key local employers, and much now hangs on the extent to which the partnership can assist in ensuring that the jobs created by a major new employer are accessed by local people and especially by those most disadvantaged in the local labour market.

This is an issue in which the BRUTEC partnership in Brussels can demonstrate some success, by identifying new job opportunities associated with new technologies and making them accessible to the young unemployed with low qualifications. Over the seven years of BRUTEC's operation, over 70% of the young people undergoing training have found work in relevant occupations, and there has also been a marked impact on the attitudes of participating employers to taking on those trained, overcoming reluctance to employ certain migrant groups. However the partnership recognises that the scale of its operation is limited, and is 'only a drop in the ocean' in relation to the needs in the wider labour market.

Other partnerships have found it much more difficult to make an impact on unemployment, although this was a significant objective. While the Paul and Tallaght partnerships have been successful in a number of respects, their impact on unemployment has been limited, and they are increasingly having to recognise that many of the important determinants of unemployment lie outside their remits and localities. Another important factor has been the limits to the active involvement of employers, due both to the small number of significant local firms and the difficulties which all local partnerships tend to face in making links to companies outside the area which might provide jobs.

Some LEADER partnerships in rural areas appear to have had considerable success in stimulating local entrepreneurship in areas where this has traditionally proved difficult and where local cultures of dependence on state welfare have been regarded as entrenched. This success, as was noted in Chapter 5, can be attributed to a number of factors, including the way in which LEADER funding is used flexibly to help generate and support local initiative. However the fact that projects needed matching funding to obtain LEADER support meant that the programme favoured those with access to capital. Consequently the case studies of some local partnerships, such as that in South Kerry, suggests that local LEADER projects may not have improved the position of the most disadvantaged groups.

b) Impact on social service provision

Those local partnerships which focused on social provision show that partnership can bring about significant improvements in social facilities and services. Thus the Paul Partnership in Limerick, the partnership in Se and S Nicolau in Porto, and the Social Services and Healthcare Districts in the Tyrol have been able to improve service delivery through more effective collaboration between partner organisations (and, sometimes, different parts of the same organisation), and as a result of the 'voice' given to users and local communities.

The partnership in Beringen supported by the Poverty 3 programme claimed several important tangible impacts as a result of the development by the partnership of a global local anti-poverty strategy: the renovation and reallocation of buildings and the creation of some 150 jobs; the development of a social enterprise project; stabilisation of the number of those entitled to receive the minimum subsistence income. The ARCIL partnership has been notably successful in bringing together local voluntary and community associations and public services to create a stronger infrastructure and facilities for those with disabilities. The partnership in Hanko in Finland claimed a notable success in reducing youth crime through the implementation of a more active, innovative and concerted approach.

c) Multidimensional partnership strategies

The research shows that in many cases local partnerships have achieved maximum impact through a broad, multidimensional approach tackling both the economic and social dimensions of exclusion.

The *Onyar Est Partnership* in Girona, Spain, achieved particular success in mobilising a large number of the city's players and sectors who had previously had little involvement in combating poverty and social exclusion. In particular, the partnership achieved a notable advance in moving from a primarily social agenda to action against unemployment, with excellent results in labour market integration as a result of the development of effective engagement of employers.

The *Ökospeicher* partnership in Wulkow represents a remarkable example of an integrated and multidimensional approach at the very local level, which from very small beginnings is now regarded as a model for other localities in several countries.

However the research also highlights some issues about the practicality of developing very broadly-based partnership strategies. Some broad multidimensional area-based partnerships - such as that in Coventry and Warwickshire, where the partnership's local regeneration agenda includes the competitiveness of local businesses as well as the needs of deprived communities - may not give priority to issues of poverty and exclusion, when faced with difficult choices over how to deploy investment and resources, and the objectives of powerful partners. The partnerships in Mantes and El Ribeiro demonstrated that there can also be substantial practical difficulties in securing and maintaining strategic coherence in a wide multidimensional approach in contexts where collaborative relationships between local actors, and between different levels of public administration, are relatively undeveloped. This means that the experience of current programmes such as URBAN (which have been too recent to include in this research) will be of considerable interest in providing further evidence of the contribution which multidimensional local urban renewal partnerships can make to tackling poverty and exclusion.

d) Impacts on empowerment and social cohesion

Local partnerships have in many cases had a positive impact in empowering excluded groups and promoting social inclusion and cohesion in deprived areas. In some cases, of which the Wulkow Ökospeicher partnership is the most notable, the partnership initiative has been instrumental in preventing the extinction and dispersal of a local community. Other partnerships, such as the IN LOCO partnership in the rural Algarve, can claim a similar if less dramatic impact in sustaining threatened communities. Numerous partnerships, the research shows, have contributed to local social solidarity, by the involvement of local communities and disadvantaged groups in decision making (Lille City Contract), or to building greater trust between authorities and groups such as young people (Iisalmi, Finland). Partners in the ARCIL partnership reflected the positive changes in attitudes that can be associated with the involvement of excluded groups:

"you come to understand that it is not people who are deficient, it is the facilities available to them that are"........and.........."you realise that people with special needs are not marginal: it is society which marginalises them".

Although by no means all of the partnerships claim a significant impact in this respect, some of the longer established partnerships, such as the Paul Partnership in Limerick, have made substantial contributions to building stronger community networks and enhancing the capacity of local community organisations. The experience of the IN LOCO partnership reflects particularly clearly the experience of many of the partnerships: that this is a long term process, which requires coherent, consistent and patient work.

e) Impacts and outcomes

The research therefore provides important evidence of the positive impacts of many local partnerships. It should be noted, however, that in some cases views on the impact of partnerships differed. In the Se and S Nicolau partnership in

Porto, for example, some leading actors emphasised the concrete actions which the partnership had undertaken. Others however wanted to give more weight to the way in which the 'galloping deterioration' of the area was outstripping the positive impact of the partnership; and the way in which "although the project had been set up to combat exclusion, there were cases in which it had actually worked as an exclusion factor, by restricting the inclusion of partners or moderating the actions of existing partners" (Rodrigues and Stoer 1996). This illustrates the fact that, while a local partnership may achieve demonstrable **impacts**, the eventual **outcome** in the local area may be less clear. In Mantes, some of those involved concluded that, although the partnership had implemented numerous projects, "the quality of life of Mantois residents, particularly those with the most serious problems, does not appear changed". The partnership in Beringen in Belgium is a similar case in point. Here the development of more collaborative relationships among local actors had several beneficial impacts: social exclusion has now become an integral issue in local politics; it has gained a wide degree of political support with the development of wider political perspectives; and the local initiative has stimulated other developments within the wider region. However, as a consequence some local actors feel that they are now being asked to assume responsibilities for social exclusion which should really be those of the provincial authorities.

Conclusion

This chapter has shown that local partnerships can have an **impact** on both the **processes** and **outcomes** of policies to tackle unemployment, poverty and exclusion:

- Local partnerships can make an important contribution to more effective local policy processes. Partnerships can lead to better policy co-ordination and integration. They can promote positive change in the approach of other local actors, accessing new resources and making better use of them, and stimulating innovative policy approaches.

- Where partnerships work effectively in such ways, the research has illustrated how partnership programmes and projects can have significant impacts on problems of unemployment and exclusion, complementary to the role of mainstream policies, through job creation, training, stimulation and support of local enterprise; improved and better targeted social services and facilities; and by involving and empowering local communities and excluded groups.

- Local partnerships which have achieved successes in these respects have had a wider impact on national and European policies.

The research has helped to identify some of the partnerships which may be considered as models of good practice, and some ways in which the achievements of local partnerships can be evaluated. However, the research also demonstrates:

- that it cannot be assumed that partnerships will always work effectively: some partnerships have achieved considerably more than others;

- that partnership working involves substantial challenges, which need to be taken into account in developing new policy programmes;

- that the timescale within which the benefits of partnership are likely to be achieved is more extended than has been recognised;

- that more attention and resources need to be devoted to the monitoring and evaluation of the impact of local partnerships, and to the 'benchmarking' and transfer of innovation and good practice.

Chapter 7	# The Contribution of Local Partnerships to Social Inclusion and Local Development: Conclusions and Proposals for Action

Introduction

This final chapter has four main purposes.

1. It begins by briefly reviewing the **key points** from the previous chapters of the report.

2. Next, it summarises what the research has found about the **strengths and limitations of local partnerships** as a method of combating exclusion, promoting local development and building a more cohesive and inclusive society.

3. Having demonstrated the utility of partnerships - in a wide variety of settings - to tackle many issues in a more comprehensive, integrated and innovative way, it is concerned with **the way forward**. A number of key issues are identified which need to be addressed to consolidate the benefits from partnerships.

4. The **implications for action** are then set out, in a way which reflects both current differences on the ground in the Member States, and the respective competencies and responsibilities of the main actors - public authorities, social partners, voluntary and community organisations, national governments and the European Union.

This report started from the recognition that local partnerships are becoming an increasingly important element of policy responses to social exclusion. It has described the way in which a partnership approach has become increasingly important in European Union policies, and has gained the support - albeit with certain reservations - of the social partners and other interested parties at European level.

This research has shown the diversity of the partnership approach. Some governments and regional authorities have supported local partnerships through national policy programmes which have paralleled European Union programmes and initiatives. In other Member States such programmes have been absent and a local partnership approach has not so far become a significant way of tackling unemployment, poverty and exclusion.

The research has identified and studied a large number of local partnerships across the countries of the EU (particularly in the ten Member States in which the research studies have been undertaken), using a working definition of local partnership which was developed in order to provide clarity and coherence in a situation in which the term 'partnership' is used in such different ways across the Union. Local partnership is clearly a flexible tool which has been developed in a wide range of geographical and socio-economic contexts, including both urban and rural areas and in locations ranging from small neighbourhoods or villages to the regional level. Local partnerships have been the result of a combination of local initiative and external stimulus from national or European programmes. The research identified many partnerships with a broad range of partners, but overall something of a 'ladder' of involvement appears to exist, with the public sector being most strongly and frequently involved, while the involvement of the social partners and the voluntary and community sectors is a feature of many partnerships but is less universal. While a significant number of the partnerships have developed a multidimensional strategy against unemployment, poverty and exclusion, others have a more defined remit concerned with employment and labour market interventions, social service delivery, and/or the multiple needs of specific social groups.

The research has described how local partnerships have combined the resources of different partners and developed and implemented significant local programmes of activity. It has shown how partnership needs to be built at both a strategic or policy level - in partnerships' management boards and committees - and at the practical, operational level of programme/project implementation. The contribution of partnerships' project teams are particularly important. Partnerships are seldom a partnership of equals, but must identify and express the expectations of all partners. The research points to the importance for local partnerships of building relationships not only 'horizontally' between local actors (where forging links between the formal partnership and more informal local networks is emphasised) but 'vertically' with national and European stakeholders. It shows that numerous partnerships have worked very effectively, but also illustrates the problems and obstacles which many have encountered, in some cases with the result that effective partnership working has failed to emerge or survive an initial experiment.

By negotiating common strategies between the public sector, the social partners and the voluntary and community sectors, local partnerships extend the tradition of social partnership in the European social model. Partnerships, the research demonstrates, can produce better co-ordinated and integrated local policy action against unemployment, poverty and social exclusion. They can be sources of policy innovation and can lever in new resources for local programmes and projects. These potential benefits, however, do bring associated challenges. In partnerships with more substantial and complex programmes, transaction costs can be high and bureaucracy can become an issue. The development of new partnership structures is leading to innovative new forms of local governance, but this is also raising questions about accountability and transparency. While local partnerships augment the capacity of local actors to tackle problems of social exclusion, this must complement, not replace, the role of national governments and public authorities.

By improving the effectiveness of local policy processes, many partnerships can demonstrate positive impacts on problems of unemployment, poverty and social exclusion, in some cases through a broad, multidimensional approach but in others by a more targeted strategy. However there has been insufficient monitoring and evaluation of the impacts and outcomes of local partnerships to permit as clear a demonstration as would be desirable of what works and what does not.

Strengths and limitations of local partnership

The research has been concerned to identify the specific added value which partnerships can bring in promoting a more cohesive and inclusive society, alongside other forms of policy intervention. The conclusions from the research can best be summarised by identifying both what benefits local partnerships can achieve, and what they cannot. The national research reports in the main conclude that the contribution of a partnership approach is most likely to be effective within the context of a continuing commitment to a universal public welfare system, to which there remains strong public attachment (Abrahamson 1996; Eurobarometer 1994). This conclusion is particularly associated with those Member States which have developed more comprehensive welfare systems, but it is also expressed in the context of other countries where public welfare provision is less universal but is an important aspiration. It is within a strong public welfare system that public agencies can make the strongest contribution in a partnership framework, and the contributions of other partners can most effectively complement public responsibilities and resources.

Within the broader frameworks of economic development, social and welfare policies, partnerships add a new dimension at the regional and local levels. Partnerships mostly work best in well defined geographical areas with specific identities. Partnerships can enable welfare systems and other policies to respond more effectively to local concentrations of unemployment, poverty and exclusion, by enhancing other policy approaches.

- Partnerships can help to develop a **collaborative culture** in a locality or region, through their enabling function of mediating and negotiating common perspectives among different interests.

- Partnerships provide a local institutional framework which can *involve and empower* key actors, including **local community interests and excluded groups**, in addressing collective issues of local development, social cohesion and inclusion.

- Local partnerships can improve the **delivery** of policies at the local and regional levels, in some cases by the direct implementation of significant integrated programmes, in others as agents and intermediaries, improving the interface between key actors.

- This can enhance the **performance** of mainstream economic, welfare and environment policies by tailoring them to local needs and capacities, and introducing a greater degree of differentiation, specificity and **responsiveness** to the needs of vulnerable social groups; and in relation to specific social problems such as crime and alcohol/substance abuse.

- Local partnerships have a **learning** function. They can act as forums for **innovation** and experimentation.

- Partnerships can enhance the **value** obtained from resources, both by applying resources more effectively in local contexts, and by levering in additional resources, both monetary and otherwise.

- Local partnerships can play valuable roles as **'advocates'** for the interests of an area, by acting as a 'spokesbody', drawing on their capacity to speak for a range of local interests in influencing policies nationally and at European level.

However, the research also makes it clear that local partnerships are not a replacement for mainstream policies.

- Local partnership, by itself, is a **valuable but not sufficient answer** to localised problems of poverty and exclusion. The more that problems in local areas are structural - rooted, for example in major weaknesses of the local economy and employment prospects, in severe deficiencies in the physical and social infrastructure, or in the poor performance of mainstream policies - the less likely is it that local partnerships will be able, by themselves, to provide solutions. Such structural issues may well be beyond the remit or competence of local partnerships.

- Partnerships have been instituted as **responses** to the problems in **specific local areas**, and often **as experimental or model actions**. They are often established on a short-term basis. They do not exist in all areas, and are unlikely to do so. Competitive bidding processes adopted in both EU and some Member State programmes confirm the selective nature of partnership initiatives, and mean that the partnership approach is not necessarily focused on areas of greatest need. Moreover, this research shows that partnerships are very hard to establish in local contexts where a supportive socio-political environment does not exist.

- Finally, the area-based nature of local partnerships means that local partnerships do not help to tackle more dispersed problems of exclusion, such as the problems of excluded groups within largely prosperous areas.

The way forward: Key issues

What, then, needs to be done, both to support and extend the benefits which many local partnerships are already bringing to efforts to tackle economic and social exclusion, and to overcome some of the barriers and limits to the impact of the partnership approach? The research identifies six key issues which need to be addressed to ensure that the gains from partnership are sustained, both by local partnerships themselves and by policymakers at national and European levels responsible for relevant programmes.

a) Representation and communication

Local partnerships can create an alliance of actors, and a culture of local solidarity, which can greatly enhance the prospects for tackling problems of poverty and social exclusion, and which are effective vehicles for implementing policy programmes and projects.

But many local partnerships face a major challenge of engaging with local communities, and especially with the most disadvantaged groups and their needs. The research highlights the need for disadvantaged groups to be offered effective representation within partnership structures and full involvement in the partnership's activity alongside other partner interests. Local partnerships which have been most successful in involving and empowering community interests have often been those where formal partnership structures are strongly rooted in the wider and more diffuse patterns of collaboration and networking between local organisations and in local communities.

Many local partnerships also need to develop clearer principles for the way in which partner interests are represented within partnership structures, and forge better links and communication between the partnership itself and partners' organisations, by clarifying mechanisms for reporting and feedback. Partner organisations also need to institute better procedures to consider the implications of partnership objectives and activity and take appropriate action.

b) Organisational capacity and skills.

Many of the national research reports call for the allocation of greater resources for capacity building and skill development for partnership working. In countries where there are currently no national programmes to support local partnerships - including Austria, Finland, Greece, Germany - the research reports recommend that national government should provide resources to promote partnership working. In countries where such programmes do exist, the research studies propose the extension of current support for local partnerships. It is also considered that EU programmes should devote more resources to supporting the building of local partnerships themselves, as well as to funding action programmes. The research has shown that project teams play a crucial role in local partnerships, but that more often needs to be done to ensure that they possess the necessary range of professional, managerial, and communication skills. There needs to be appropriate provision of training and development for partnership staff and others involved which reflects the specific challenges and demands of partnership activity and enables those working in partnerships to respond flexibly to the changing needs of programmes and projects. The implications of this are discussed further below.

c) Financial resources

The research shows clearly that the short-term funding - typically lasting from three to five years - provided by most national and European Union programmes, is seldom if ever sufficient to allow partnership relationships to become securely rooted, not only in the partnership itself but also in partner organisations. Ad hoc solutions have been found to sustain successful local partnerships over a longer period of time, by successive allocations of funding from different sources. But many partnerships have failed to achieve this, and even where they have, experience suggests that the management of a succession of short-term funding sources poses serious problems for partnerships in terms of insecurity and adjustment to different regimes

d) Timescales

There is much evidence from the national research reports and other research on these issues (Ball 1994; OECD 1997b) to suggest that the problems of poverty and exclusion with which local partnerships are contending are not susceptible to solution through short term interventions. Local partnerships have mostly had the status of pilot or experimental actions, or time-limited interventions, dependent on short term funding, even when they have been supported by large scale national or EU programmes. In some countries, the emphasis on the short-term nature of partnerships has been reinforced by government concern with the development of 'exit strategies' for the termination of partnership funding. Partnership takes a considerable time to develop and secure relations of trust, collaboration and reciprocity. If partners, including local communities and excluded groups, are to make the heavy investments of time, work and learning necessary, this requires confidence that the benefits from such investments can be realised. Short-term investment often represents poor or wasted use of resources by governments, the EU and other partners. The conclusions from the EU's Poverty 3 programme were that the five year horizon of the projects was more relevant to the demonstration of the *potential* of local partnership than to the achievement of long-term results (Estivill et al 1994). The recent LEDA review of partnership (Humphreys 1996) appears to assume that partnerships need to be permanent, or at least long-term.

These considerations raise important questions for future European and national programmes supporting local partnerships. To what extent should partnerships become a more permanent part of the institutional framework of policy to combat poverty and exclusion, and of local governance? Are local partnerships **transitional** arrangements - promoting policy innovation, contributing to solutions to specific local problems of poverty and exclusion, but then giving way to 'mainstream' agencies and policies - or more **permanent** elements of new policy frameworks?

e) Transparency and accountability

The research shows that, as local partnerships become more established tools of policy, issues of transparency and accountability are becoming of greater significance. Several dimensions of this issue have been identified in this research:

- the individualised nature of the representation of interests in local partnerships, and the limited degree to which effective and transparent means of reporting back to partner organisations and constituencies have been instituted,

- the uni-directional, top-down nature of accountability relationships and limited transparency within partnership programmes,

- the 'paradox' in some partnerships between effective collective action by partner organisations from the public, private and voluntary sectors but a lack of involvement of excluded communities and groups themselves, which can reinforce the polarisation between the excluded and mainstream society,

- the tensions which can emerge between local partnerships and the 'mainstream' representative democratic process.

These findings suggest that attention will need to be given to ways of avoiding a potential 'democratic deficit' as a result of local partnership, while retaining its benefits. The implication from the research is that the development of local partnerships is leading to a tension between three potentially conflicting principles of local democracy, which need to be effectively reconciled. One is the traditional principle of representative democracy, in which local elected representatives play the pivotal role. The second is the principle of participative democracy, through the direct involvement of other actors, including excluded groups and communities, in local partnerships. The third is the pluralist principle of interest group representation, which is also critical to the makeup of many local partnership structures. The research suggests that what is needed is to exploit opportunities to combine the virtues and avoid the limitations of these three principles in partnership working.

f) Research, evaluation and dissemination

The limited extent of monitoring, evaluation and research in many partnerships is hindering their effectiveness, by failing to provide adequate feedback on their progress and impact, and is making it difficult for national and European policy makers, and others, to assess the advantages and disadvantages of the many 'models' of local partnership which are associated with different EU, national and local initiatives. At the same time, those involved in partnerships at the local level often feel that national and European programmes do not offer adequate opportunities for exchange of experience and learning between local partnerships, and the dissemination of good practice both nationally and transnationally, or at the local level itself. There is a need for further research on the methods, techniques and tools of evaluation most appropriate to local partnerships.

The implications for action

Some of the implications for the future development of local partnerships depend on the way in which a partnership approach has developed in the national contexts of different Member States. In national contexts where local partnerships are already an important element in the policy response to unemployment, poverty and social exclusion, the need is often for the consolidation of the gains from partnership. In other national contexts, where the local partnership approach is less widespread, or has failed to take root, the need is for an appraisal and review of the ways in which the local partnership approach can be adjusted to national and local contexts. Each of the national reports (see Appendix I) makes specific recommendations for the way forward in the Member State concerned.

However, important general implications for action can also be drawn from the research concerning the strengthening of the contributions of the different stakeholders.

The role of public authorities

One of the most important factors which has determined the extent to which a local partnership approach has developed as part of the response to problems of poverty and exclusion is whether or not national and regional governments have instituted programmes which are implemented at local level on a partnership basis. Programmes, such as the Contrat de Ville in France, City Challenge in the United Kingdom, the Social Renewal programme in the Netherlands, the Local Enterprise and Integrated Development programmes in Ireland, and the Fund to Stimulate Social Action in Flanders, have supported many of the local partnerships analysed in this research.

The research indicates that national and/or regional governments should have regard to a number of **principles** in developing the framework of policy within which local partnerships can make the most effective contribution to tackling problems of poverty and exclusion.

- National and/or regional governments should institute programmes which fund and support local partnerships.

- These programmes should be closely linked to mainstream social and economic policies.

- Local experience and conditions should be taken into account in the development and implementation of national and regional programmes.

- Within wider programmes for urban and regional regeneration or local economic development, there need to be explicit guidelines and objectives to ensure that issues of poverty and exclusion are given priority.

- The development of national strategies or frameworks to promote local development and social cohesion can provide a coherent context for local partnership activity.

- National and regional programmes should offer local partnerships adequate guarantees of the longer-term support needed to achieve impacts, provided partnerships are able to demonstrate good progress in relation to agreed shorter term targets.

- National and/or regional policy programmes must ensure that local partnerships have access to the **expertise, skills, time** and **resources** which they need. In particular, support from programmes should be available for the following:

  * Development of **management competencies** for partnerships. Those involved in partnerships require a specific set of skills to manage complex projects and promote communication and understanding

between partners. If local partnerships are to attract and retain suitable staff, consideration also needs to be given to the implications of partnership for the **career patterns and training** of managers and staff.

* **Community development and capacity building.** While resourcing is needed to support the capacity of all partners to contribute effectively to local partnerships, the greatest need remains to support the active and positive involvement of community organisations and excluded groups. This is likely to require systematic national funding of community development programmes, often of a long term nature, to enable community organisations to better research and represent local needs. This may best be provided through specialist national agencies.

* **Evaluation**. Programmes must promote an evaluative culture in local partnerships, which combines a concern for positive outputs with a formative role in developing effective working processes. This should involve shared responsibility for target setting and evaluation between those responsible for national/regional programmes and local partnerships themselves. Provision also needs to be made within national programmes for the exchange of experience between those involved in partnerships at the local level, and for this local knowledge to be fed back into national policy.

• National and regional governments must ensure that **gender and equal opportunity** perspectives are built into programmes supporting local partnerships. This is likely to include:

* Requiring local partnerships to give priority to equal opportunity issues in their strategies and action plans.

* Requiring local partnerships to recognise equal opportunity considerations in developing the structure and working processes of the partnership, through the development of a 'quota' approach or other means.

* allocating specific resources to achieve these objectives, and making provision for monitoring and evaluating the results and disseminating good practice.

The development of stronger and more supportive national and regional frameworks for local partnerships may involve some direct expenditure, but would help to ensure that much greater 'added value' is achieved from investment at the local level, with fewer failures and waste of resources, including the attraction of higher levels of funding 'levered in' from other partners and sources alongside public investment.

The public sector often has a dominant influence on the way in which most local partnerships work, reflecting its primary responsibilities in this policy area. National, regional and local public authorities and agencies play a leading role in many local partnerships, which in turn depends on the contribution of public policies in maintaining levels of social service provision and expenditure, and the development of local infrastructure.

However, while partnership requires a strong public sector, this must also be open and accountable, subject to democratic control, and willing and able to engage positively with local and other partners. Local partnership often seems to work better in a decentralised state structure which offers a high degree of autonomy to local and regional levels of government.

A more effective public sector contribution to local partnerships would therefore be enhanced by:

- The extension of a 'community governance' approach by public authorities at the local level. This implies a recognition, of the leading role of local government not just in delivering services but in exercising local leadership in the community.

- The development of a more co-ordinated approach among national government ministries and agencies, especially between economic and social policy responsibilities, to enable national agencies to play a more coherent role in local partnerships.

- Better 'vertical' partnership between national, regional and local state agencies, according to principles of subsidiarity.

- A better defined role for elected local representatives on partnership management bodies, with support available from public authorities for local politicians playing an active role in local partnerships, so that local democratic accountability is strengthened rather than weakened by partnership working.

- The development or extension of training and capacity building for individuals from public agencies involved in local partnerships, including senior professionals, officials and elected politicians.

The voluntary and community sectors

The active involvement of local community interests, including the participation of the most excluded groups, has been identified by the research as a crucial element of local partnership. However, the extent of representation, and of effective influence and power, of community and social interests is very varied. Some of the case studies offer instances where marginalised communities lead local initiatives; but in most community involvement, and particularly that of the most excluded, is limited or non-existent. If partnership is to be more than 'partnership from above' - a closed shop for policy elites and formal organisations, and especially if it is to engage with the excluded themselves, then:

- An **active network** of voluntary and community organisations, especially those providing a channel for the aspirations of excluded social groups and communities, is necessary.

- This requires long-term financial and other **resources** to support the process of building the capacity of community organisations, as has been argued by other research for the Foundation (Chanan 1992 and 1997).

- At the same time, the involvement of voluntary and community sector organisations carries with it enhanced responsibilities. There is a need for some voluntary and community organisations to institute more **open and democratic procedures** for their own conduct, and enhance their representative base, if they are to sustain their claims to speak and act on behalf of their members or constituencies in partnership contexts.

- Organisations representing the voluntary and community sector at the European level, such as the European Anti-Poverty Network, can play an important role in facilitating and promoting the more effective involvement of community interests in local partnerships.

Employers

Employers and employer organisations play important roles in many local partnerships. But the research shows that in many Member States the contribution of employers could be considerably greater than it is at present.

- If employers are to make a stronger contribution to local partnerships, there is a need for individual employers or employer representatives on partnership bodies to adopt a more representative stance on behalf of the local business 'community', and for local employer organisations to foster more effective means of communication between the individuals on partnership bodies and the wider business community.

- If local partnerships are to address issues of unemployment and social exclusion effectively, this would require the business community to embrace a social agenda within their local areas. While employers cannot avoid the constraints which the need to remain competitive imposes, the research shows numerous examples of ways in which this is consistent with active involvement with other partners in promoting local development and social cohesion. These range from financial and other support to social projects for excluded groups, to recruitment and employment policies which give greater priority to those disadvantaged in the labour market.

- Initiatives such as the European Declaration of Businesses against Exclusion and the European Business Network for Social Cohesion, and the recent Danish government conference (October 1997) on a 'New Partnership for Social Cohesion' show how examples of greater involvement by employers can be disseminated at national and European levels.

- More active involvement of employers in local partnerships needs to be supported by advice and training, including provision by employers themselves through their national and European organisations.

Trade unions

As is the case with employers, there is considerable potential for more active trade union participation in local partnership. The research indicates that in several countries trade unions are now increasingly reaffirming a stronger concern with the social and political dimension and are bridging the gap between the representation of the interests of workers and the common interests of all citizens. In Greece for example, the creation of a Fund for Employment and Vocational Training is a recent product of a new momentum of social dialogue and collaboration by the social partners on programmes to assist excluded groups most disadvantaged in the labour market. A recent report from an OECD trade union expert group (OECD 1996), points out that if the trade unions are not proactive, the vacuum will be filled by other interests.

- At national level, trade unions should take a more proactive approach to involvement in local partnerships, building positive working relations at local level with other interests, including voluntary and community organisations representing excluded groups. This would strengthen their ability to speak and work for all workers, including the unemployed and excluded. Active involvement in partnerships could strengthen trade union membership by making them more useful and attractive to their members, and broadening their social profile.

- Increased involvement in local partnerships will require support and training for trade union representatives from their unions and national trade union organisations.

- The ETUC should play an important role in promoting the inclusion of trade union interests as an integral element of local partnership in EU programmes, and in disseminating experience of the advantages of trade union participation on a transnational basis.

European Union policies and programmes

The research confirms the importance of EU policies in promoting and supporting local partnerships. This contribution has been significant especially in countries where it has not developed actively through local initiative or national programmes, such as Greece, and parts of Portugal and Spain. However in these countries the impact of EU programmes still does not yet appear to have been sustained or substantial enough to have succeeded in fully 'rooting' local partnership principles in the national policy community. In other Member States, such as the UK, Germany and France, the impact of EU initiatives has been limited by the small scale of EU funding compared to national programmes and policies. EU interventions have had the most positive impact in Member States such as Ireland where national and EU policies have been closely aligned and where the scale of Structural Fund intervention is more significant in the national context.

The research has been able to evaluate the experience of a significant number of local partnerships which have participated in EU Community Initiatives and social action programmes. A number of conclusions can be drawn from this comparative dimension of the research.

- The research shows that there is no one 'blueprint' for local partnerships. This suggests the importance of continued support from the EU for the **transnational exchange of experience and good practice** between local partnerships supported by different EU initiatives, by national programmes, and by local initiative. This needs to be 'mainstreamed' in the design of programmes and projects. Transnational monitoring, evaluation and benchmarking is assuming increasing importance as the number of programmes supporting local partnerships increases. This transnational exchange would be of benefit to national policymakers, other stakeholders and local partnerships themselves.

- The **timescales** for building local partnerships and achieving benefits are longer than the four or five years which are typical of funding programmes. While many successful partnerships have succeeded in attracting further funding after the expiry of initial support, the uncertainty engendered, and the need to reorient objectives and structures in line with new funding, can pose major problems. A new balance may therefore need to be achieved between the short and long term if partnerships are able to develop secure and effective strategies, and the costly and discouraging high 'mortality rate' of partnerships is to be reduced.

- A particular finding from the research concerns the positive effect in **stimulating local initiative** and **attracting matching funding** which was achieved in some LEADER I partnerships as a result of funding arrangements which encouraged a flexible and responsive use of resources. This approach could be applied elsewhere, in urban as well as rural contexts.

- The research has shown that in many cases effective **'horizontal' partnership** at the local level needs to be supplemented by **'vertical' partnership** between local actors, regional and national authorities and the EU itself. In particular, the positive ways in which local partnerships have succeeded in co-ordinating and integrating different policy domains, especially economic and social policies and objectives, supports the current concern for better co-ordination between the different European Commission services with responsibility for economic and social policies.

- **Equal opportunities and local partnerships**. The Commission's 1996 Report on Equal Opportunities for Women and Men in the European Union (European Commission, 1997) commits the Union to the 'mainstreaming' of equal opportunity in European Union policies, so that the gender dimension of policies is taken into account systematically both in respect of the impact of policies and the decision-making process. This research confirms that there is a need for such a 'mainstreaming' in EU programmes encouraging the development of local partnerships. This report has pointed to examples of such 'mainstreaming', but there is a need for this experience to be adopted more widely to ensure equality of opportunity. The EU can play a vital role in this respect by demonstrating best practice through its own policies and initiatives and thus influencing national and local partnership-based programmes.

Partnerships and the review of cohesion policy. The research has relevance to the current review of structural policies and the cohesion objective now being conducted by the European Union. The European Commission's own conclusions, as expressed in the First Report on Economic and Social Cohesion, and those of many other parties contributing to the recent Cohesion Forum held in Brussels in May 1997, indicate the widespread conviction, as expressed by one contributor to the Forum, that '**partnership is at the heart of the delivery of EU Structural Funds**' (Brady 1997).

This is reflected, first, in the Commission's recognition of the need to strengthen partnership arrangements within the Monitoring Committees, including a clearer distinction between consultation of partners and involvement in decision making. The definition of partnership adopted for this research confirms the need to make such a distinction between a general 'partnership approach' and the specific contribution of local partnerships which implement strategies, programmes and projects 'on the ground'.

Secondly, the Commission's review of the Structural Funds is suggesting a need for more effective targeting of resources to areas of need. This approach is supported by the findings of this research that problems of unemployment, poverty and exclusion often need to be given higher priority where local partnerships have a broad remit to promote local development and regeneration.

Thirdly, this research shows the desirability of drawing on the experience of more successful local partnerships, in determining the future role of local partnerships in EU programmes. This may require a more sophisticated and differentiated approach to the requirements for partnership in different contexts. In some Member States where the partnership principle is well established, the requirement for a working partnership as a precondition for participation in EU programmes may well be effective, but in other Member States the research suggests that more time and resources may need to be devoted to the establishment of working local partnership if such partnerships are to survive and prove effective mechanisms for policy and programme delivery.

Finally, this research echoes and reinforces the findings of the Commission's review of cohesion policy concerning the need for more substantial exchange of experience programmes, dissemination of local best practice, and the 'mainstreaming' of innovation pioneered at the local level. Specific European resources will be needed to undertake this and to develop appropriate tools for the purpose.

Conclusion

Local partnership is now seen as an important element of the way forward in European Union policies and programmes, and those of many Member States, which are tackling problems of unemployment, poverty and social exclusion. The objectives of this research have been to analyse the way in which the local partnership approach is being adopted, to assess the impact of local partnerships, and to develop guidelines and recommendations to assist policy makers and others in the future. It is hoped that the results of the research will enable lessons to be learned from the experience of the many local partnerships which have been investigated. They show that building local partnership, and securing the greatest benefits from partnership working, poses significant challenges both to policy makers and to all those involved in partnerships at the local level. But where local partnerships are able to meet these challenges, they can contribute to the emergence of a more active and inclusive society and to what may be termed a 'negotiated economy', in which consensus-creating institutions form one of the keys to economic prosperity.

Appendix I

National Research Reports and other supplementary research papers available from The European Foundation for the Improvement of Living and Working Conditions

Kain E and Rosian I, The role of partnerships in promoting social cohesion: Research report for Austria. WP/96/31/EN.

Carton B, Delogne R, Nicaise I and Stengele A, The role of partnerships in promoting social cohesion: Research report for Belgium. WP/96/32/EN.

Heikkila M and Kautto M, The role of partnerships in promoting social cohesion: Research report for Finland. WP/96/36/EN.

Le Gales P and Loncle P, The role of partnerships in promoting social cohesion: Research report for France. WP/96/37/EN.

Birkholzer K and Lorenz, G, The role of partnerships in promoting social cohesion: Research report for Germany. WP/96/33/EN.

Robolis S, Papadogamvros V, Dimoulas K and Sidira V, The role of partnerships in promoting social cohesion: Research report for Greece. WP/96/30/EN.

Walsh J, Craig S and McCafferty D, The role of partnerships in promoting social cohesion: Research report for Ireland. WP/96/38/EN.

Rodrigues F and Stoer S M with Vaz H., The role of partnerships in promoting social cohesion: Research report for Portugal. WP/96/35/EN.

Estivill J with Nartinez R, The role of partnerships in promoting social cohesion: Research report for Spain. WP/96/34/EN.

Geddes M with Benington J, The role of partnerships in promoting social cohesion: Research report for the United Kingdom. WP/95/29/EN.

Other research reports prepared in the course of the research are:

Geddes M, The role of partnerships in promoting social cohesion: Discussion paper WP/95/38/EN.

Benington J and Geddes M, The role of partnerships in promoting social cohesion: The European Union dimension (Unpublished).

National research reports are also available in the national language.

APPENDIX II

a) The National Research Teams

Austria

Eva Kain and Ingrid Rosian
Österreichisches Bundesinstitut für Gesundheitswesen
Stubenring 6
A - 1010 Wien   Tel: +43 1 5156161
Austria   Fax: +43 1 5138472

Belgium

Ides Nicaise, Bruno Carton
Roger Delogne and A Stengele
Katholieke Universiteit Leuven
Hoger Instituut voor de Arbeid
E Van Evenstraat 2e
B - 3000 Leuven   Tel: +32 16 323337
Belgium   Fax: +32 16 323344

Finland

Matti Heikkilä and Mikko Kautto
STAKES
National Research and Development Centre
for Welfare and Health
Siltasaarenkatu 18C, PO Box 220
FIN - 00531 Helsinki   Tel: +358 9 39672211
Finland   Fax: +358 9 39672007

France

Patrick le Galès and Patricia Loncle
Centre de Recherche Administrative et Politique
Université de Rennes
104 Boulevard de la Duchesse Anne
F - 35700 Rennes Cedex   Tel: +33 99843904
France   Fax: +33 998843900

Germany

Karl Birkhölzer and Günther Lorenz
Lokale Ökonomie
c/o Technische Universität Berlin, Sekt FR 4-8
Interdisziplinares Forschungs Projekt
Franklinstraße 28/29
D - 10587 Berlin   Tel: +49 30 31473394
Germany   Fax: +49 30 31421117

Greece

Savas Robolis, Vasilis Papadogamvros,
Kostas Dimoulas and Vivi Sidira
University of the Aegean
71A Emm. Benaki Street
GR - 106 81 Athens   Tel: +30 1 3304469-474
Greece   Fax: +30 1 3304452

Ireland

Jim Walsh, Sarah Craig and Des McCafferty
Combat Poverty Agency
Bridgewater Centre
Conyngham Road
Islandbridge
Dublin 8   Tel: +353 1 6706746
Ireland   Fax:: +353 1 6706760

Portugal

Fernanda Rodrigues and Steven Stoer
ADEF
Rua do Rosario
110 - 2° Dto
P - 4050 Porto   Tel: +351 2 200 24 54
Portugal   Fax: +351 2 200 24 54

Spain

Jordi Estivill and Raul Martinez
Gabinet d'Estudis Socials
Arago 281 2n2a
E- 08009 Barcelona   Tel: +34 3 4873816
Spain   Fax: +34 3 2158815

United Kingdom

Mike Geddes and John Benington
The Local Government Centre
Warwick Business School
University of Warwick   Tel: +44 1203 522458 - Mike
Coventry, CV4 7AL   Tel: +44 1203 524505 - John
England   Fax: +44 1203 524410

The research for the five other member states was undertaken by N Bosco, Dipartimento di Scienzi Sociale, University of Turin (Italy), M Dahlstrom, European Institute of Social Services, University of Kent (Sweden), C Olsen, Centre for Alternative Social Analysis, Copenhagen (Denmark), S Serail IVA Tilburg, Institute for Social Research (Netherlands) and M Geddes, University of Warwick (Luxembourg).

b) Co-ordination Group

Stefanos Lemos
Representative of EF Administrative Board
(Unions Group)
General Confederation of Greek Workers
Patission & Pipinou 27   Tel: + 30 1 8202273
GR - 102 10 Athens   Fax: + 30 1 8202186/87/90
Greece

Bernard Le Marchand
Representative of EF Administrative Board
(Employers Group)
Conseiller de la Fédération Européenne des
Moyennes et Grandes Enterprises (FEMGED)
Avenue Victor Gilsoul 76
B - 1200 Brussels   Tel: + 32 2 7715871
Belgium   Fax: + 32 2 7715871

William Jestin
Representative of EF Administrative Board
(Government Group)
Department of Enterprise and Employment
Davitt House
65 A Adelaide Road
Dublin 2   Tel: +353 1 6614444
Ireland   Fax: +353 1 6769047

Jos Jonckers
Directorate-General V
Commission of the European Communities
200, rue de Loi (J-27 1/04)
B - 1049 Brussels   Tel: + 32 2 2953047
Belgium   Fax: +32 2 2990509

Stefaan de Rynck
Directorate General XVI,
Commission of the European Communities
200 rue de la Loi (CSM2-02-101)
B- 1049 Brussels   Tel: +32 2 2966721
Belgium   Fax: +32 2 29 66229

Christina Theochari
EF Committee of Experts
Department of the Environment
Athens Labour Centre
48B, 3rd September Street
GR - 10433 Athens   Tel: +30 1 8839271
Greece   Fax: +30 1 8836917

c) Research Managers

Wendy O'Conghaile and Robert Anderson
European Foundation for the Improvement of Living and Working Conditions.

APPENDIX III   Local Partnerships In The European Union

(Case studies are highlighted)

Country	Name	Location	Origins	Funding	Issues	Partners
AUSTRIA	Women's Foundation Steyr	Urban / rural	Self-help initiative, national government.	Employment Service, Provincial government, Federal government, European Social Fund.	Female Unemployment	Women from trade unions, local authority, Provincial and Federal government, quasi-public body (Employment Service), regional social partners, private sector.
	Social Services and Health Care District 'Regions 12 and 13' Tyrol	Rural	Local politicians, private citizens, Provincial government.	Provincial government, local authority, social security bodies, donations, fees paid by service-recipients.	Social and medical provision, family support, poverty, women, health promotion.	Provincial government, local authority, voluntary sector, local community, private sector.
	Korneuburg Social Area	Urban	Provincial government, local authority, Employment Service.	Provincial government, local authority, Employment Service.	Social and medical provision, unemployed, women, foreigners, homeless people.	Provincial government, local authority, quasi-public bodies, voluntary sector, local community, private sector.
	Employment Initiatives by local authorities in the District of Bruck/Mur	Rural (former industrial area)	Local authorities, Employment Service.	Local authorities, Provincial government, Employment Service.	Unemployment, regional development, women, young people's housing problems.	Local authorities, Provincial government, quasi-public body (Employment Service), social partners (employer and employee bodies), private sector.

Country	Name	Location	Origins	Funding	Issues	Partners
AUSTRIA	"Quality of Life Workshop", Linz	Urban	Federal government	Local authority, Federal government, private research institute.	Quality of life, environment, women, children, sick persons and those in need of help and care.	Local authority, Federal government, private research institute, local community, private sector, voluntary sector.
	Carinthian Labour Foundation Programme	Urban, rural	Regional social partners, national government.	Provincial government, Employment Service, European Social Fund, Austrian Economic Chamber.	Unemployment, vocational training, regional development.	Trade union, employee and employer bodies, provincial government, quasi-public body (Employment Service), private sector.
BELGIUM	Vlaams Fonds voor de Integratie van Kansarmen (VFIK) (Beringen)	Urban	Regional	Regional authorities	Poverty, immigrants.	Local authorities, Centres Publics d'Aide Sociale (CPAS), voluntary sector.
	Training islands: 'Working with groups at risk' (Antwerp)	Urban	Local authorities, trade unions, employers.	Chamber of Commerce, regional authorities.	Unemployment, training.	Chamber of Commerce, voluntary sector, private sector.
	Action for social co-ordination (La Louviere)	Urban, rural	Regional	Regional authorities	Networks between social workers, poverty.	Local authorities, social workers from public and voluntary sector.
	Employment fund: a partnership for groups at risk	Urban	Interprofessional agreement between social partners at federal level	Levy on wage bill, European Social Fund.	Training, employment.	Employers, trade unions, public training agencies.
	Fund to promote integration and coexistence between local communities	Urban	Regional (Brussels Region)	Regional authorities	Citizenship, coexistence with immigrants, social integration.	Local authorities, voluntary sector, local community.

Country	Name	Location	Origins	Funding	Issues	Partners
BELGIUM	Fund to combat social exclusion in the Walloon region	Urban, rural	Regional (Walloon Region)	Regional authorities, local authorities.	Poverty, delinquency, training.	Local authorities, professionals.
	Partnership agreements	Urban	Regional (Brussels Region)	Regional authorities, European Social Fund.	Training, employment.	Centres Publics de 'Aide Sociale (CPAS), voluntary sector, public training agency.
	Charleroi pilot project: 'To win with the losers'	Urban	EU Poverty 3	EU Poverty 3, regional and local authorities.	Poverty, unemployment, health.	Local authorities, trade unions, voluntary sector, local community, employers.
	BRUTEC: Association Bruxelloise pour la Formation aux Nouvelles Technologies et la Promotion de l'Emploi	Urban	Voluntary sector	Regional authorities, European Social Fund.	Unemployment, training.	Local associations, regional authorities, trade unions, employers.
	Summer programme for young people: 'Blé-jeunes'	Urban	Regional	Regional authorities	Social integration, participation of young people.	Local authorities, voluntary sector.
DENMARK	Enterprise Mon	Rural	Local organisations	Ministry of Social Affairs	Employment, economic development.	Local authority, employers, trade unions, community organisations.
	Vapnagard Urban Commission Model Project	Urban (suburb)	Ministry of Social Affairs, Helsingør municipality.	Ministry of Social Affairs	Coordinated economic social and cultural development	Municipality, housing association, tenants, other local organisations.
	Rita's Corner	Urban	Local voluntary sector	Ministry of Social Affairs, local authorities.	Psycho-social care services	Association for the Mentally Ill, local authorities.

Country	Name	Location	Origins	Funding	Issues	Partners
FINLAND	Vuosaari	Urban	Local	Municipality, Ministry of Environment.	Housing, environment, social cohesion.	Municipality, residents association, Ministry of Environment.
	Sirkkulan-puisto	Urban	Grassroots	RAY (the Slot Machine Association)	Alcohol abuse, housing, life control, employment.	Municipality, regional government, Ministry, university, RAY (voluntary association).
	Kemijärvl	Rural	Local	Ministry of Employment, municipality.	Rehabilitation, education, employment.	Municipality, employment agency, Social Insurance institution, adult training centre, association for the disabled, private sector.
	Joutseno	Urban (de-industrialised)	Local (with national connections)	RAY, Ministry of Education, Ministry of Employment.	Education, employment.	Municipality, local employers, Mannerheim League for child welfare.
	Iisalmi	Urban	Grassroots	Ministry of Trade, Ministry of Employment, Finnida, European Social Fund.	Education, employment, development aid, life planning.	Municipality, voluntary organisation, vocational training institute, local organisation of unemployed.
	Hanko	Urban (de-industrialised)	Local	Municipality	Juvenile delinquency, employment, education.	Municipality, police, mental health centre and clinic, parish, local employment agency.
	Hämeenkyrö	Rural	National	Ministry of Social Affairs and Health, Ministry of Education.	Employment, delinquency, alcohol and drug abuse.	Municipality, employers, vocational education board, employment agency, parish.
FRANCE	LEDA Programme St Etienne	Urban, rural	EU LEDA, region.	EU, region.	Employment	Local authorities, social partners, state agencies.

Country	Name	Location	Origins	Funding	Issues	Partners
FRANCE	Poverty 3 Mantes-la-Jolie	Urban, suburb	EU Poverty 3, local	EU, local authorities.	Poverty	Local authorities
	Partenariat CFDT-CCI Rennes	Urban, rural	Local social partners	Social partners	Employment, insertion.	Local authorities, voluntary sector, social partners.
	Mission Locale Nantes	Urban environment	National government, local authorities.	National government	Employment	Local authorities, voluntary sector, social partners.
	Groupe d'Action Locale du Centre-Ouest Bretagne (GALCOB)	Rural environment	EU LEADER, region, local authorities.	EU, region.	Poverty, employment, rural development.	Local authorities, voluntary sector, social partners.
	Culture Quartiers Toulouse	Urban environment	Local voluntary sector	Local authority	Social and cultural insertion.	Local authorities, voluntary sector, state agencies.
	Coopérative Extra-Muros Lille	Urban environment	Local community	Local (public and private)	Poverty	Voluntary sector
	Contrat de Ville de Lille	Urban environment	National government, local authority.	National and local government	Social & economic insertion	Local authorities, voluntary sector, state agencies.
GERMANY	Industrielles Gartenreich Dessau	Urban, ex-industrial, rural	Bauhaus Foundation Dessau	Foundation	Rural and urban social and ecological regeneration	Public-law foundation, voluntary sector, employment agencies.
	Ökospeicher Wulkow	Rural, village	Municipality	ABM job creation programme, Federal, local.	Rural development, unemployment.	Municipality, private companies, individuals.
	LEDA Leer	Urban, rural district	EU LEDA and LEADER	EU, Land government.	Unemployment, regional economic development.	Town, district, voluntary organizations, farmers.

Country	Name	Location	Origins	Funding	Issues	Partners
GERMANY	Kommunales Forum, Wedding, Berlin	Major city (district)	Community group	ABM job creation programme, state.	Unemployment, poverty, community economic development.	Community initiatives, district, council, social enterprises.
	FNP Kiel	Urban/rural	Trade union	Regional programme, EU, own income.	Employment	City, district, trade unions, engineering consultancies.
	EWZ Dortmund	Ex-industrial conurbation	Trade union	ABM programme, EU.	Unemployment, training for the disadvantaged, cultural integration.	Town council, trade unions, social enterprises.
	Beschäftigungs verbund Heidelberg	Urban/rural	Social projects and companies	Local authority, self-generated income.	Unemployment, poverty, employment creation.	Social enterprises, social projects, town council.
	Poverty 3 Berlin - Friedrichshain	Major city (district)	Berlin Senate, EU Poverty 3.	EU, ABM programme.	Poverty, social projects.	Social initiatives, district council, social enterprises.
GREECE	West Attica Development Association	Urban	EU NOW	EU NOW, national government.	Social and economic development, education, training, psychological support.	State agencies, local authorities.
	THISSEAS Poverty 3 project	Urban (suburb of Athens)	EU Poverty 3	EU Poverty 3, national government.	Health, training, employment, drug abuse, social support.	Local authorities, local community, public authorities, municipality, voluntary sector.
	Argiroupolis Poverty 3 project	Urban (suburb of Athens)	EU Poverty 3	EU Poverty 3, national government.	Socio-economic support, business initiatives, training, consultancy.	State agencies, local authorities, voluntary sector.
	Deaf language training of trainers Horizon 1 project	Urban (suburb of Athens)	EU Horizon 1	EU Horizon, national government.	Education, training, social support for handicapped people.	Municipality, trade unions, universities.

Country	Name	Location	Origins	Funding	Issues	Partners
GREECE	Social exclusion of Muslim minorities	Urban	Voluntary initiative	European Social Fund, national government.	Social support, information, health, consultancy, training.	State agencies, municipality, voluntary organisations.
	Perama	Urban	EU Poverty 3	EU Poverty 3, national government.	Health, education and training, employment, social and economic support.	State agencies, local authorities, trade unions, voluntary organisations.
IRELAND	Tallaght Partnership	Urban	Grassroots initiative, national government.	National government, EU.	Poverty, long term unemployment.	Local and public authorities, community and voluntary organisations, trade unions, employers.
	South Kerry Development Partnership	Rural	Grassroots initiative, LEADER programme.	National government, EU LEADER.	Rural development, long term unemployment.	Local and public authorities, community, trade unions, employers.
	Pavee Point	Urban	Grassroots initiatives	National government, EU.	Travellers	Community, local and public authorities.
	Paul Partnership Limerick	Urban	Grassroots initiatives, EU Poverty 3.	National government, EU Poverty 3.	Poverty, long term unemployment.	Local and public authorities, local community, voluntary sector, trade unions, employers.
	Mallow Partnership	Urban / rural	Grassroots initiative	National government, EU.	Long term unemployment	Local and public authorities, local community, employers.
	Greater Blanch'stown Development Project	Urban	Church	National government	Poverty	Local community, local and public authorities.
	Dundalk Employment Partnership	Urban	National government	National government, EU, International Fund for Ireland.	Long term unemployment	Local and public authorities, local community, trade unions, employers.

Country	Name	Location	Origins	Funding	Issues	Partners
IRELAND	Ballymun Task Force	Urban	Grassroots initiative	National government	Public housing, environment.	Politicians, local authorities, public agencies, community.
ITALY	Centre for the Prevention of Juvenile Crime, Siracusa	Urban	Local organisations	National	Juvenile crime	Local authority, local voluntary and community organisations, trade unions.
	Alma Mater Centre, Turin	Urban	Women trade unionists	Commune of Turin, Region of Piedmont, EU NOW.	Immigrant women	Local authorities, local voluntary and community organisations, trade unions.
NETHERLANDS	Workcentres (Rotterdam, Den Helder, Hengelo, Eindhoven)	Urban	Local public agencies	Local and national authorities, EU, local partners.	Social and employment services for the long term unemployed	Local authorities, employers' associations, local trade unions.
	Neighbourhood Management (Deventer and Nijmegen)	Urban	Local authorities	Local authorities	Urban renewal and services	Local authorities, residents' groups and organisations.
PORTUGAL	Solidários Cooperative and Community Development Foundation (Aveiro)	Rural	Community initiative	National government, EU .	Training, unemployment, rural development, information.	Local authorities, voluntary organisations, local associations.
	Raizes para um futuro de sucesso (Setubal)	Urban	Public department of Social Security	National government, local sources.	Poverty, social exclusion, housing, health, education, training.	State agencies, local authorities, voluntary sector.
	Projecto Zona Histórica Sé e S. Nicolau (Porto)	Urban	National government, EU Poverty 2.	EU Poverty 3, Horizon, NOW, Euroform, National anti-poverty programme.	Poverty, housing, education, training, unemployment, health, social facilities.	Government departments, voluntary associations and organisations, local authorities, cultural and sports associations.

Country	Name	Location	Origins	Funding	Issues	Partners
PORTUGAL	Associação IN LOCO Algarve	Rural	Local Community initiative	EU LEADER, LEDA, National programme.	Education, rural development, training, social and economic facilities.	Local authorities, public administration, local associations, employers' associations.
	Mundo Rural em Transformação (Guarda)	Rural	Voluntary organisations, EU Poverty 2 and 3.	EU Poverty 3, NOW, Horizon, Euroform, INTERREG, National programme.	Poverty, rural development, education and training.	Public departments, local authorities, local firms, local associations.
	Escola Profissional Braga	Urban	National programme	European Social Fund, National programme.	Vocational education, unemployment.	Public department, local authorities, employers' associations.
	Empresa da Messejana para o Desenvolvimento Comunitário (Messejana)	Rural	Local community initiative	EU LEADER, European Social Fund, National anti-poverty programme.	Rural development, training, unemployment, education.	Local authorities, public department, associations of employers, farmers and artisans.
	ARCIL - Associaçaõ para a recuperação de Cidadaõs Inadaptados da LOUSÃ	Rural and urban	Local community initiative	EU Helios, Horizon. National anti poverty programme.	Special needs, education, health, social facilities, employment.	Local authorities, employers, public department.
	Acçáo modelo Desenvimento Comunitario de Pombal	Rural / urban	Public department, EU Poverty 2.	EU Poverty 3, European Social Fund, National programme.	Single parents, housing, health, employment, elderly.	State department, local authorities, voluntary organisations, employers associations.
SPAIN	El Ribeiro	Rural	Regional government, EU INTERREG, local initiatives.	National, regional and local government.	Underdevelopment, exclusion.	Regional and local administration, local initiatives.

Country	Name	Location	Origins	Funding	Issues	Partners
SPAIN	Girona	Urban	Local administration, EU Poverty 2&3.	EU Poverty 2&3, national, regional and local governments.	Poverty, socio-economic integration.	3 levels of public administration, trade unions, local multinational employers, grass roots initiatives, NGOs.
	Plan Vasco, Alava, Basque Country	Urban (area of old industrialization)	Regional government	Regional and provincial governments, EU Poverty 3.	Poverty, minimum income coordination.	Regional, provincial and local administration.
	Montes de Oca	Rural	Local authorities	National, regional and local governments.	Rural development	National, regional and local administrations, trade unions, employees, local initiatives.
	Traperos	Urban	Grassroots initiatives	Local funds, EU Horizon.	Extreme poverty,	Local foundation
	Alta Muntanya	Rural	Regional and local authorities	Regional and local authorities	Rural development	Regional and local administration, other local partners.
SWEDEN	Fryhuset (The Freeze house)	Urban	Local community	Public agencies and other local partners	Young people	Community organisations and activists, local public authorities, employers.
	Norrkoping Business Network	Urban	Various local partners	Local partners	Employment for people with disabilities	Public and private employers, regional social insurance office, trade unions.
	Gothenburg City Mission Foundation	Urban	Local voluntary sector	Local voluntary sector and other local partners	Services to homeless, drug and alcohol abusers.	Voluntary organisation, public sector agencies.
UNITED KINGDOM	Western Isles and Skye & Lochalsh LEADER	Remote rural	Public agencies, EU LEADER.	EU LEADER, other public and private sector.	Rural development and enterprise, cultural regeneration.	Public & quasi - public agencies, farmers' organisations, NGO.

Country	Name	Location	Origins	Funding	Issues	Partners
UNITED KINGDOM	South Pembrokeshire Partnership for Action with Rural Communities	Rural	Local, organisations, EU LEADER.	EU LEADER, local partners.	Rural community development, business development, rural tourism, environmental improvement.	Public & quasi - public agencies, community organisations.
	Rotherham Community & Economic Regeneration Partnership	Urban & rural coalfield	Local government	Local authority	Employment and economic development, poverty, housing, community development.	Local government, local public & quasi-public agencies, national agencies, local community, voluntary sector.
	North Tyneside City Challenge Partnership	Urban (old industrial region)	Local government, local community, national government (City Challenge).	National government (City Challenge) and associated funding	Economic development, physical regeneration, social regeneration.	Local government, local public and quasi-public agencies, voluntary sector, private sector, local community.
	Granby-Toxteth Community Project	Urban (inner city)	Local community and agencies. EU Poverty 3.	EU Poverty 3	Poverty, unemployment, housing, community development, ethnic groups.	National and local government, local community, university, church groups, employers (limited).
	Coventry and Warwickshire Partnerships Ltd	Urban and rural (city region)	Local government, local public agencies.	National government (Single Regeneration Budget)	Economic and social regeneration	Local government, local public and quasi - public agencies, private sector, voluntary sector, community organisations & groups, trade unions.
	Castlemilk Partnership, Glasgow	Urban (conurbation)	Local community, local and national government.	Central and local government, private sector.	Economic development, housing, environment, education, social improvement.	National government (Scottish Office), local public and quasi-public agencies, private sector, local community, voluntary sector.

Country	Name	Location	Origins	Funding	Issues	Partners
UNITED KINGDOM	Brownlow Community Trust	Urban/peripheral region	Grassroots / community initiative, EU Poverty 3 .	EU Poverty 3	Poverty, unemployment, housing, health, education, community development.	Public agencies, local community, employer (limited).

Appendix IV

Acronyms used in the Report

ADAPT	EU Community Initiative for the adaptation of the workforce to industrial change
ADM	Area Development Management (Ireland)
ARCIL	Associaçaõ para a recuperação de adadaõs inadaptos de Lousa (Portugal)
BRUTEC	Association Bruxelloise pour la Formation aux Nouvelles Technologies et la Promotion de l'Emploi (Belgium)
CEC	Commission of the European Communities
CEEP	Centre European de Employeurs Publics
CFDT	Confederation de Travail (France)
COFACE	Confederation of Family Organisations in the European Community
COR	Committee of the Regions
CPAS	Centres Publiques d'Aide Sociale (Belgium)
DSQ	Developpement Social des Quartiers (France)
EC	European Commission
ECOSOC	Economic and Social Committee
EFILWC	European Foundation for the Improvement of Living and Working Conditions
ESF	European Social Fund
ETUC	European Trade Union Congress
ETUI	European Trade Union Institute
EU	European Union

EWZ	Entwicklungszentrum, Dortmund (Germany)
FNP	Förderverein Neue Produktion, Kiel (Germany)
GALCOB	Group d'Action Locale du Centre Ouest Bretagne (France)
GDP	Gross domestic product
GNP	Gross national product
HORIZON	EU Community Initiative (Employment) for people with disabilities.
ILO	International Labour Office
IN LOCO	Local development association, Algarve, Portugal
INTEGRA	EU Community Initiative (Employment) for people threatened with social exclusion
INTERREG	EU Community Initiative for cross-border collaboration
LASAIRE	Laboratoire Social D'Actions D'Innovations et de Reflexions et d'Echanges (France)
LEADER	EU Community Initiative for rural development
LEC	Local Enterprise Company (UK - Scotland)
LEDA	Local Employment Development Action Programme (DGV)
NGO	Non-governmental organisation
NOW	New Opportunities for Women (EU Social Action Programme)
OECD	Organisation for Economic Co-operation and Development
RAY	National slot machine association (Finland)
SKDP	South Kerry Development Partnership (Ireland)
SME	Small and medium enterprises
SRB	Single Regeneration Budget (UK)
UK	United Kingdom
UNICE	Union of Industrial and Employers' Confederations of Europe
URBAN	EU Community Initiative for regeneration of crisis-struck areas in medium and large-sized towns
VFIK	Vlaams Fonds voor de Integratie van Kansarmen (Belgium)
WISL	Western Isles and Skye and Lochalsh (LEADER I partnership)

Bibliography

Abrahamson P 1996: *A framework for rethinking social welfare systems*. Paper to conference on New Directions in Social Welfare, Dublin, 14-16 November, organised by the Department of Social Welfare and the European Foundation for the Improvement of Working and Living Conditions.

Abrahamson P and Hansen FK 1996: *Poverty in the European Union*. European Parliament.

Brady S 1997: *Developing Structural Fund Partnerships*. European Cohesion Forum, Working Documents, Brussels: European Commission.

Bruto da Costa A 1994: *The Contribution of Poverty 3 to the Understanding of Poverty, Exclusion and Integration*, EEIG Animation & Recherche, Lille.

CEEP 1994: *European Declaration of Business against Exclusion*, European Centre of Enterprises with Public Participation.

Chanan G 1992: *Out of the Shadows: Local community action and the European Community*. Dublin: European Foundation for the Improvement of Living and Working Conditions. Luxembourg: Office for Official Publications of the European Communities.

Chanan G 1997: *Active Citizenship: Getting to the Roots*. Dublin: European Foundation for the Improvement of Living and Working Conditions. Luxembourg: Office for Official Publications of the European Communities.

Commission of the European Communities 1989: 'Medium Term Community Action Programme to Foster the Economic and Social Integration of the Least Privileged Groups', *Bulletin of the European Communities*, Supplement 4/89, Brussels.

Conroy P 1994: *Evaluation of the Achievements of Poverty 3, Synthesis. Contributions to the preparatory work for the White Paper on European Social Policy*, Social Europe Vol 2 DGV.

Council of the European Union 1997: *Treaty of Amsterdam* amending the Treaty on European Union and the Treaties establishing the European Communities and certain related acts. Luxembourg: Office for Official Publications of the European Communities.

Cousins M 1997: *New Directions in Social Welfare: Report of a conference of the Irish Presidency of the European Union.* Dublin: European Foundation for the Improvement of Living and Working Conditions. Luxembourg: Office for Official Publications of the European Communities.

Deakin N, Davis A and Thomas N 1995: *Public welfare services and social exclusion: The development of consumer-oriented initiatives in the European Union.* Dublin: European Foundation for the Improvement of Living and Working Conditions. Luxembourg: Office for Official Publications of the European Communities.

Denmark, Ministry of Social Affairs 1996: *A New Partnership for Social Cohesion.* Copenhagen: Ministry of Social Affairs.

Estivill J et al 1994: *Partnership and the Fight Against Exclusion*, Poverty 3, EEIG Animation et Recherche, Lille.

ETUI, 1993: *The European Structural Funds in the Regions: Experiences of Trade Union Participation.* ETUI 331.88, Brussels.

European Business Network for Social Cohesion 1996: *Corporate Initiatives: Putting into practice the European Declaration of Businesses against Exclusion.* Brussels: King Baudouin Foundation.

European Commission 1993a: *European Social Policy : Options for the Union*, DGV, COM (93) 551.

European Commission 1993b: *Growth, Competitiveness, Employment. The Challenges and Ways Forward into the 21st Century. White Paper.* Luxembourg: Office for Official Publications of the European Communities.

European Commission, 1994a: *European Social Policy - A way forward for the Union (White Paper)*. Luxembourg: Office for Official Publications of the European Communities.

European Commission 1994b: *Local Development Strategies in Economically Disintegrated Areas: A Pro-Active Strategy Against Poverty in the European Community*. Final report June 1994. European Commission Social Papers 5.

European Commission 1994c: *The Perception of Poverty and Social Exclusion in Europe 1994*. Eurobarometer, DGV.

European Commission 1995a: *European Strategy for Encouraging Local Development and Employment Strategies*, COM (95) 273 final.

European Commission 1995b: *Medium -Term Social Action Programme 1995-97*, COM (95) 134 final, Social Europe 1/95, DGV.

European Commission 1995c: *Proposal for a Council Decision on the Commission's activities of analysis, research, cooperation and action in the field of employment (ESSEN)*. COM (95) 250 final.

European Commission 1995d: *The Future of Social Protection: A framework for European debate*. Brussels: European Commission COM (95) 466 final.

European Commission 1996a: *Report of the European Social Policy Forum*, Brussels, March 1996.

European Commission 1997a: *First report on Economic and Social Cohesion 1996*. Luxembourg: Office for Official Publications, of the European Communities.

European Commission 1997b: *Equal Opportunities for Men and Women in the European Union 1996*. Luxembourg: Office of Official Publications.

European Commission 1997c: *European Cohesion Forum, Working Documents, Workshop I, (Partnership)*. Brussels.

European Commission 1997d: *Modernising and Improving Social Protection in the EU*. COM (97) 102, Brussels.

European Commission 1997e: *Employment in Europe 1996*. Luxembourg: Office for Official Publications of the European Communities

European Communities, Economic and Social Committee, 1993a: *Social Exclusion, Opinion*, Brussels.

European Communities, Economic and Social Committee, 1993b: *Medium Term Community Action Programme to Foster the Economic and Social Integration of the Least Advantaged Groups, Opinion*, Brussels.

European Communities, Economic and Social Committee 1997: *Opinion on the First Cohesion Report*. Brussels.

European Parliament 1997: *Assessment of the EU's Structural Expenditure: Part II: Social policy expenditure*. Luxembourg: European Parliament: Directorate General for Research.

EUROSTAT 1997: *Income distribution and poverty in the EU 12 - 1993*. Luxembourg: Office for Official Publications of the European Communities.

Griffiths J 1995: *Business and Social Exclusion, A Guide to Good Practice*, A Report for the London Enterprise Agency Conference, London, British Telecom.

Henderson P 1997: *Social Inclusion and Citizenship in Europe: The contribution of community development*. Den Haag: Combined European Bureau for Social Development.

Humphreys E 1996: *LEDA Local Pilot Actions: Synthesis Report*, for European Commission, Directorate General for Employment, Industrial Relations and Social Affairs.

LASAIRE 1995: *Combating Social Exclusion in Europe and Creating Integrated Labour Market Entry Schemes*, Proceedings of European Seminar, Lille.

Leigh-Doyle S and Mulvihill R 1996: *Social Exclusion: A major challenge for the public welfare services*. Dublin: European Foundation for the Improvement of Living and Working Conditions. Luxembourg: Office for Official Publications of the European Communities.

Nicaise I and Henriques J-M (Eds) 1995: *Trade Unions, Unemployment and Social Exclusion*, Proceedings of European Seminar, Hoger Instituut voor de Arbeit, KU Leuven.

OECD Labour Management Programme 1997: *The role of trade unions in local development: Report of a meeting of trade union experts*. Paris: OECD.

OECD Territorial Development Service, Urban Affairs Division, forthcoming: *Distressed Areas Study*. Paris: OECD.

■

Robbins D 1992: *Observatory on national policies to combat social exclusion, Third Annual Report.* Lille: EEIG.

Robbins D (Ed) 1994: *Observatory on national policies to combat social exclusion, Third Annual Report,* Lille: EEIG.

Room G (Ed) 1995: *Beyond the Threshold: The Measurement and Analysis of Social Exclusion,* Policy Press, Bristol.

Sabel C 1996: *Ireland: Local Partnerships and Social Innovation.* Paris: OECD.

UNICE 1997: *UNICE Position paper on the First Report on economic and social cohesion in the European Union.* European Cohesion Forum, Working Documents. Brussels: European Commission.

European Foundation for the Improvement of Living and Working Conditions

Local Partnership: A Successful Strategy for Social Cohesion?

Luxembourg: Office for Official Publications of the European Communities

1998 – 181 pp. – 16.0 cm x 23.5 cm

ISBN 92-828-3050-0

Price (excluding VAT) in Luxembourg: ECU 40